3

CONTEMPORARY TOPICS

Academic Listening and Note-Taking Skills

THIRD EDITION

David Beglar
Neil Murray

Michael Rost
SERIES EDITOR

PEARSON
Longman

Contemporary Topics 3
Advanced
Academic Listening and Note-Taking Skills
Third Edition

Copyright © 2009 by Pearson Education, Inc.

Pearson Education, 10 Bank Street, White Plains, NY 10606

Staff credits: The people who made up the *Contemporary Topics 3* team, representing editorial, production, design, and manufacturing, are Rhea Banker, Danielle Belfiore, Dave Dickey, Christine Edmonds, Nancy Flaggman, Dana Klinek, Amy McCormick, Linda Moser, Carlos Rountree, Jennifer Stem, Leigh Stolle, Paula Van Ells, Kenneth Volcjak, and Pat Wosczyk.
Cover design: Rhea Banker
Cover art: © Jennifer Bartlett, Detail of *Rhapsody*. Photo: Geoffrey Clements/Corbis
Text composition: Integra Software Services, Pvt. Ltd.
Text font: Times 11.5/13
Credits: See page 133.

Library of Congress Cataloging-in-Publication Data
Beglar, David.
Contemporary topics 3 : academic listening and note-taking skills / David Beglar, Neil Murray.—3rd ed.
  p. cm.
Rev. ed. of: Contemporary topics 3—advanced listening and note-taking skills.
ISBN-13: 978-0-13-234523-1
ISBN-10: 0-13-234523-4
1. English language—Textbooks for foreign speakers. 2. Listening. 3. Listening comprehension.
4. Note-taking—Study and teaching. I. Murray, Neil (Neil L.) II. Beglar, David.
Contemporary topics 3—advanced listening and note-taking skills. III. Title. IV. Title:
Contemporary topics three.
PE1128.B4189 2009
428.3'4—dc22

2008049656

PEARSON LONGMAN ON THE WEB

Pearsonlongman.com offers online resources for teachers and students. Access our Companion Websites, our online catalog, and our local offices around the world.

Visit us at **www.pearsonlongman.com**.

Printed in the United States of America
7 8 9 10—V042—13 12

CONTENTS

SCOPE and sequence

UNIT SUBJECT AND TITLE	CORPUS-BASED VOCABULARY		NOTE-TAKING AND LISTENING FOCUS	DISCUSSION STRATEGIES	PROJECT
1 **COMMUNICATION STUDIES** **Slang and Language Change**	attitudes constantly construct evolving expanding	identity inevitable phenomenon reinforces widespread	Sequence markers to organize your notes	■ Agreeing ■ Asking for clarification or confirmation ■ Paraphrasing	Researching slang terms
2 **CHILD PSYCHOLOGY** **The Genius Within**	devoted exhibit inconsistencies motivation	predominant strategy underlying	Examples	■ Offering a fact or example ■ Asking for clarification or confirmation ■ Asking for opinions or ideas	Researching someone who is gifted and presenting
3 **SOCIOLOGY** **Social Status: Flaunting Your Success**	attaining consumption global	hierarchies income status symbols	Key terms and definitions	■ Asking for opinions or ideas ■ Paraphrasing ■ Keeping the discussion on topic	Researching a status lifestyle and presenting
4 **BUSINESS** **The Art of Marketing in a Global Culture**	enables guaranteed ideological	media promote	Symbols and abbreviations	■ Expressing an opinion ■ Disagreeing ■ Offering a fact or example	Researching an advertisement and presenting
5 **COGNITIVE PSYCHOLOGY** **Memory**	chemicals decade implicit logical manipulate	psychologists release retain temporarily	Cause-and-effect relationships	■ Expressing an opinion ■ Offering a fact or example ■ Keeping the discussion on topic	Researching a memory improvement technique and presenting
6 **ANTHROPOLOGY/ BIOLOGY** **The Science of Love**	attachment enhance invoke	mutual prospective	Lists	■ Asking for opinions or ideas ■ Disagreeing ■ Trying to reach a consensus	Discussing how love is presented in a novel or film

UNIT SUBJECT AND TITLE	CORPUS-BASED VOCABULARY		NOTE-TAKING AND LISTENING FOCUS	DISCUSSION STRATEGIES	PROJECT
7 ASTRONOMY Mission to Mars	detecting facilities maintain resources	sustainable unreliable vehicle	Organization	■ Expressing an opinion ■ Disagreeing ■ Keeping the discussion on topic	Researching a space mission and presenting
8 POLITICAL SCIENCE Big Brother and the Surveillance Society	civil controversial security	techniques via	Numbers and statistics	■ Agreeing ■ Asking for clarification or confirmation ■ Trying to reach a consensus	Researching surveillance opportunities or developments and presenting
9 LINGUISTICS Animal Communication	discrete distinct flexible generation	precise random ultimately	Comparisons and contrasts	■ Expressing an opinion ■ Agreeing ■ Asking for clarification or confirmation	Researching animal communication and presenting
10 ECONOMICS The Evolution of Money	abandoned abstract currency	enormous initiative undergone	Marking your notes	■ Expressing an opinion ■ Agreeing ■ Offering a fact or example	Speculating on how money will change and presenting
11 BIOLOGY The Fountain of Youth	accumulate benefit function	plus supplement	Problem-solution relationships	■ Asking for opinions or ideas ■ Disagreeing ■ Asking for clarification or confirmation	Researching an approach to human life extension and presenting
12 SOCIOLOGY Marriage	adulthood confirmed couples	matured norm	Personal reactions to topics	■ Expressing an opinion ■ Offering a fact or example ■ Paraphrasing	Discussing qualities necessary for a successful marriage

ACKNOWLEDGMENTS

The series editor, authors, and publisher would like to thank the following consultants, reviewers, and teachers for offering their invaluable insights and suggestions for the third edition of the *Contemporary Topics* series.

Kate Reynolds, *University of Wisconsin-Eau Claire*; Kathie Gerecke, *North Shore Community College*; Jeanne Dunnett, *Central Connecticut State University*; Linda Anderson, *Washington University in St. Louis/Fontbonne University*; Sande Wu, *California State University, Fresno*; Stephanie Landon, *College of the Desert*; Jungsook Kim, *Jeungsang Language School*; Jenny Oh Kim, *Kangnamgu Daechidong*; Stephanie Landon, *Bunker Hill Community College*; Kathie Gerecke, *North Shore Community College*; Patty Heiser, *University of Washington*; Carrie Barnard, *Queens College*; Lori D. Giles, *University of Miami*; Sande Wu, *California State University, Fresno*; Kate Reynolds, *University of Wisconsin-Eau Claire*; Nancy H. Centers, *Roger Williams University*; Lyra Riabov, *Southern New Hampshire University*; Jeanne Dunnett, *Central Connecticut State University*; Dr. Steven Gras, *ESL Program, SUNY Plattsburgh*; series consultants Jeanette Clement and Cynthia Lennox, *Duquesne University*

In addition, the authors of *Contemporary Topics 3* would like to thank Michael Rost, Leigh Stolle, and Amy McCormick for their unwavering support during the development of the book. Their insight, experience, and creativity have been invaluable in helping shape and polish it, and their patience and understanding during periods of "overload" was greatly appreciated. Finally, we would like to thank Averil Coxhead for allowing us the use of the Academic Word List, and all those who, whether formally or informally, took the time to share their thoughts about the book and their suggestions as to how we might improve *Contemporary Topics 3*.

INTRODUCTION

Content-based learning is an exciting and effective way for students to acquire English. The *Contemporary Topics* series provides a fresh content-based approach that helps students develop their listening, note-taking, and discussion skills while studying interesting, relevant topics.

The *Contemporary Topics* series appeals to students in many different contexts because it utilizes a variety of multimedia technologies and caters to a range of learning styles. The *Contemporary Topics* series is ideal for students who are preparing to study in an English-speaking academic environment. It's also suitable for all students who simply wish to experience the richness of a content-based approach.

Each unit centers around a short academic lecture. Realistic preparation activities, focused listening tasks, personalized discussions, challenging tests, and authentic projects enable students to explore each topic deeply.

The lecture topics, drawn from a range of academic disciplines, feature engaging instructors with live student audiences, and take place in authentic lecture hall settings. The multimodal design of each lecture allows for various learning formats, including video- and audio-only presentations, optional text subtitling, optional Presentation Points slide support, and for DVD users, optional pop-up Coaching Tips. In the student book, the 🎧 and 👁 icons indicate that the activity requires either the CD or the DVD.

In order to achieve the goals of content-based instruction, the *Contemporary Topics* series has developed an engaging eight-step learning methodology:

STEP 1: CONNECT to the topic   *Estimated Time: 10 minutes*

This opening section invites students to activate what they already know about the unit topic by connecting the topic to their personal experiences and beliefs. Typically, students fill out a short survey and compare answers with a partner. The teacher then acts as a facilitator for students to share some of their initial ideas about the topic before they explore it further.

STEP 2: BUILD your vocabulary   *Estimated Time: 15 minutes*

This section familiarizes students with some of the key content words and phrases used in the lecture. Each lecture contains 10–15 key words from the Academic Word List to ensure that students are exposed to the core vocabulary needed for academic success.

Students read and *listen to* target words and phrases in context, so that they can better prepare for the upcoming lecture. Students then work individually or with a partner to complete exercises to ensure an initial understanding of the target lexis of the unit. A supplementary Interact with Vocabulary! activity enables students to focus on form as they are learning new words and collocations.

STEP 3: F O C U S *your* attention *Estimated Time: 10 minutes*

In this section, students learn strategies for listening actively and taking clear notes. Because a major part of "active listening" involves a readiness to deal with comprehension difficulties, this section provides specific tips to help students direct their attention and gain more control of how they listen.

Tips include using signal words as organization cues, making lists, noting definitions, linking examples to main ideas, identifying causes and effects, and separating points of view. A Try It Out! section, based on a short audio extract, allows students to work on listening and note-taking strategies before they get to the main lecture. Examples of actual notes are also provided in this section to give students concrete "starter models" they can use in the classroom.

STEP 4: L I S T E N *to the* lecture *Estimated Time: 20–30 minutes*

As the central section of each unit, Listen to the Lecture allows for two full listening cycles, one to focus on "top-down listening" strategies (Listen for Main Ideas) and one to focus on "bottom-up listening" strategies (Listen for Details).

In keeping with the principles of content-based instruction, students are provided with several layers of support. In the Before You Listen section, students are guided to activate concepts and vocabulary they have studied earlier in the unit.

The lecture can be viewed in video mode or listened to in audio mode. In video mode, the lecture includes the speaker's Presentation Points and subtitles, for reinforcing comprehension (recommended as a final review). It also includes Coaching Tips on strategies for listening, note-taking, and critical thinking.

STEP 5: T A L K *about the* topic *Estimated Time: 15 minutes*

Here students gain valuable discussion skills as they talk about the content of the lectures. Discussion skills are an important part of academic success, and most students benefit from structured practice with these skills. In this activity, students first listen to a short "model discussion" involving native and non-native speakers, and identify the speaking strategies and gambits that are used. They then attempt to use some of those strategies in their own discussion groups.

The discussion strategies modeled and explained across the twelve units include asking for and sharing opinions and ideas, agreeing and disagreeing, offering facts and examples, asking clarification questions, seeking confirmation, paraphrasing, and managing the discussion.

STEP 6: R E V I E W *your* notes *Estimated Time: 15 minutes*

Using notes for review and discussion is an important study skill that is developed in this section. Research has shown that the value of note-taking for memory building is realized *primarily* when note-takers review their notes and attempt to reconstruct the content.

In this activity, students are guided in reviewing the content of the unit, clarifying concepts, and preparing for the Unit Test. Abbreviated examples of actual notes are provided to help students compare and improve their own note-taking skills.

STEP 7: TAKE *the unit* test *Estimated Time: 15 minutes*

This activity, Take the Unit Test, completes the study cycle of the unit: preparation for the lecture, listening to the lecture, review of the content, and assessment.

The Unit Test, contained only in the Teacher's Pack, is photocopied and distributed by the teacher, then completed in class, using the accompanying audio CDs. The tests in *Contemporary Topics* are intended to be challenging—to motivate students to learn the material thoroughly. The format features an answer sheet with choices. The question "stem" is provided on audio only.

Test-taking skills include verbatim recall, paraphrasing, inferencing, and synthesizing information from different parts of the lecture.

STEP 8: EXTEND *the* topic *Estimated time: 20 minutes minimum*

This final section creates a natural extension of the unit topic to areas that are relevant to students. Students first listen to a supplementary media clip drawn from a variety of interesting genres. Typically, students then choose an optional extension activity and prepare a class presentation.

By completing these eight steps, students gain valuable study skills to help them become confident and independent learners. The *Contemporary Topics* learning methodology and supporting multi-media package help students to develop stronger listening, speaking, and note-taking skills and strategies.

A supplementary **Teacher's Pack** (TP) contains Teaching Tips, transcripts, answer keys, and tests. The transcripts include the lectures, the student discussions, the test questions, and audio clips from Focus Your Attention and Extend the Topic. Full transcriptions of the DVD Coaching Tips and Presentation Points are available online at:

www.pearsonlongman.com/contemporarytopics

We hope you will enjoy using this course. While the *Contemporary Topics* series provides an abundance of learning activities and media, the key to making the course work in your classroom is student engagement and commitment. For content-based learning to be effective, students need to become *active* learners. This involves thinking critically, guessing, interacting, offering ideas, collaborating, questioning, and responding. The authors and editors of *Contemporary Topics* have created a rich framework for encouraging students to become active, successful learners. We hope that we have also provided you, the teacher, with tools for becoming an active guide to the students in their learning.

Michael Rost
Series Editor

TO *the* student

Listening to lectures for the first time in English can be an overwhelming experience. This is not surprising considering the number of things you need to do during the note-taking process. First, you have to hear and understand the words the lecturer is speaking. You need to understand and consider the content itself and decide what is worth noting and what is not. Then, you need to actually write your notes in English, and as you do so, ensure they are organized in a way that makes sense to you when you come back to them later—perhaps weeks, even months later. And as you are trying to do all of this, the lecturer is not waiting for you, but continuing to talk!

Contemporary Topics 3 has been written to provide you with a number of effective listening and note-taking strategies that will make this demanding task easier, and to give you plenty of practice in applying those strategies before, during, and after you listen to the lectures on the accompanying CD/DVD. The strategies presented include predicting content, focusing on main ideas and identifying their supporting details, identifying discourse cues and the language of debate and discussion, taking good notes, and reviewing those notes effectively.

Another key to academic success is building your vocabulary. This book suggests many strategies for vocabulary-building. The Academic Word List and Affix Charts at the end of this book can give you a strong foundation in common academic vocabulary. Using both a dictionary and a thesaurus will also help.

In order to improve your learning and make the *Contemporary Topics 3* "experience" an engaging and rewarding one, we have tried to include topics that are interesting, current and varied, and in many cases, a little controversial too! We hope you enjoy using the book as much as we and the *Contemporary Topics* team enjoyed writing and recording it. Good luck!

David Beglar, Professor and Program Director of the Graduate Program in Education (TESOL), College of Education, Temple University Japan Campus

Neil Murray, Senior Lecturer and Program Director at the School of International Studies, University of South Australia

UNIT 1

Slang and Language Change

"You kids have a sick time at the party!"

CONNECT *to the* topic

Slang is an integral part of language in the twenty-first century. Young people in particular are highly creative in the way they invent and use new slang terms. Without an understanding of slang, communicating with those around us would be difficult. In fact, slang allows people to connect on a deeper level. That's why people who are learning a new language often try to "pick up" a few slang terms early on—it helps them feel like authentic speakers of the language and part of their new second-language community.

Work with a partner. List as many slang terms that you can think of. Then guess their meanings.

Slang term	Meaning
·····➤ arm candy	an attractive person who accompanies somebody to public gatherings
·····➤ _____	_____
·····➤ _____	_____
·····➤ _____	_____
·····➤ _____	_____

Choose three of the slang terms from your list and use them in sentences.

BUILD *your* vocabulary

A. The boldfaced words are from this unit's lecture on slang and language change. Listen to each sentence. Then guess the meaning of the boldfaced words. Work with a partner.

1. **Attitudes** toward slang vary widely. While some people approve of it, others are neutral or disapprove of it strongly.

2. Language never stays the same for long; it's **constantly** changing.

3. Slang helps us to **construct** friendships by showing others that we "speak their language" and are therefore part of their group.

4. The world is continually **evolving** thanks to the development of new and better technology.

5. Young people play an important role in **expanding** language by adding a variety of slang and new meanings.

6. People often try to create an **identity** for themselves by wearing a particular style of clothing or speaking in a certain way.

7. Many people think that a desire to be different is an **inevitable** part of teenage development, a natural phase teens can't avoid.

8. Language is a fascinating and unique **phenomenon**. How human language distinguishes us from other animals has been studied for years.

9. For some people, teenagers' use of slang and other forms of "bad" language **reinforces** the idea that they are rebellious and do not want to conform.

10. The use of slang was not always as **widespread** as it is today; nowadays most people use it quite freely.

B. Now choose the best definition for each boldfaced word.

1. **attitudes** vary
   a. ways of behaving
   b. personalities
   c. opinions and feelings

2. **constantly** change
   a. all the time
   b. unwillingly
   c. without thinking

3. **construct** friendships
   a. search for
   b. create or build
   c. understand
      the meaning of

4. continually **evolving**
   a. developing
   b. becoming worse
   c. going out of fashion

5. **expanding** language
   a. showing off
   b. checking
   c. increasing

6. create an **identity**
   a. a facial expression
   b. a quality that makes
      someone distinct
   c. a sense of interest

7. an **inevitable** part
   a. unavoidable
   b. important
   c. difficult

8. a **phenomenon**
   a. a human characteristic
   b. a remarkable thing
   c. an idea

9. **reinforces** the idea
   a. devalues
   b. supports
   c. creates

10. not as **widespread** as
   a. important
   b. popular
   c. common

C. *INTERACT WITH VOCABULARY!* **Work with a partner. Cover Group A as your partner reads sentences 1–5. Listen and write the missing words in Group B. Your partner corrects your answers. Switch roles for 6–10.**

Group A

1. People always try to **adapt to** their communities.

2. Slang **breeds in** groups who don't want to be understood.

3. We show our beliefs **by using** particular language.

4. Slang is **the focus of** a lot of language research.

5. Many parents aren't **in tune with** their teenagers' interests.

6. New language tends to be closely **associated with** youth.

7. Some slang is **exclusive to** particular communities.

8. **Experts in** language are often fascinated by slang.

9. Language is crucial to our **integration into** society.

10. Some social groups are **made distinct by** their unique use of language.

Group B

1. People always try to **adapt** _____ their communities.

2. Slang **breeds** _____ groups who don't want to be understood.

3. We show our beliefs _____ **using** particular language.

4. Slang is **the focus** _____ a lot of language research.

5. Many parents aren't **in tune** _____ their teenagers' interests.

6. New language tends to be closely **associated** _____ youth.

7. Some slang is **exclusive** _____ particular communities.

8. **Experts** _____ language are often fascinated by slang.

9. Language is crucial to our **integration** _____ society.

10. Some social groups are **made distinct** _____ their unique use of language.

FOCUS _your_ attention

SEQUENCE MARKERS TO ORGANIZE YOUR NOTES

Lecturers will often use sequence markers to signal when they are about to introduce the next point or part of a lecture or the next item in a list. Being able to identify these markers can help you distinguish different ideas and better organize your notes. Some commonly used sequence markers include the following:

To start / begin with, . . .

First, . . . ; Second, . . . ; Third, . . .

Next, . . .

Then . . .

Moving on . . .

Let's move on to . . .

Another point / idea . . .

Last, . . .

Finally, . . .

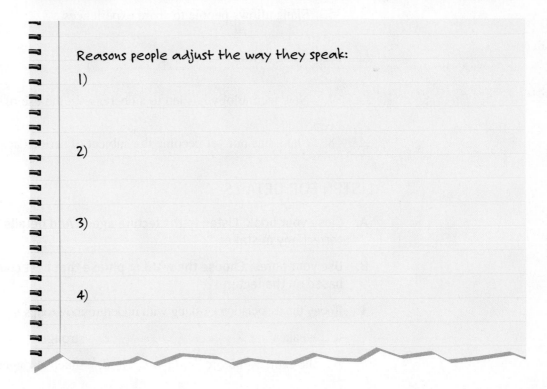

TRY IT OUT!

A. **Listen to this excerpt from a lecture on language. What sequence markers do you hear? Take notes below on the four reasons the speaker gives.**

B. **Compare your list with a partner.**

Reasons people adjust the way they speak:

1)

2)

3)

4)

LISTEN *to the* lecture

BEFORE YOU LISTEN

You are about to listen to this unit's lecture on slang. Why do you think people use slang?

_____

LISTEN FOR MAIN IDEAS

A. Close your book. Listen to the lecture and take notes.

B. Use your notes. Decide if the statements below are *T* (true) or *F* (false), according to the lecture. Correct any false statements.

____ 1. We cannot stop language change from happening.

____ 2. Slang only breeds among deprived and secretive groups.

____ 3. Slang takes away people's identity.

____ 4. Well-educated, successful people rarely use slang.

____ 5. Slang allows people to share experiences.

____ 6. Slang is fun.

____ 7. New technology has led to a decrease in the use of slang.

____ 8. Slang has not yet become the subject of serious academic study.

LISTEN FOR DETAILS

A. Close your book. Listen to the lecture again. Add details to your notes and correct any mistakes.

B. Use your notes. Choose the word or phrase that best completes each idea, based on the lecture.

1. Today the association of slang with underground groups is _____.

    a. weaker   c. stronger

    b. the same as before   d. much stronger

2. One use of slang is to _____ understanding.

   a. improve   c. prevent

   b. create   d. check

3. People who are "out-group" are _____.

   a. excluded   c. opponents of slang

   b. respected   d. poor users of slang

4. Slang can give people status if they _____.

   a. know the latest slang terms   c. avoid bad slang

   b. use it frequently   d. know how to use it

5. S. I. Hayakawa describes slang as "the poetry of everyday _____."

   a. love   c. emotions

   b. life   d. feelings and beliefs

6. One of the richest sources of slang today is _____.

   a. love and romance   c. new technology

   b. expressions of like and dislike d. websites about slang

7. Most people believe that language and literacy are _____.

   a. worsening   c. including more slang

   b. improving   d. becoming more creative

8. According to the lecture, slang _____ considered taboo.

   a. used to be   c. is still

   b. was never   d. is increasingly

9. People who dislike slang often associate it with groups who are
   _____ and _____.

   a. uneducated / criminal   c. impolite / uneducated

   b. criminal / undesirable   d. undesirable / uneducated

10. The lecturer's attitude toward language change is _____.

    a. extremely negative   c. neutral

    b. negative   d. positive

TALK *about the* topic

A. Listen to the students talk about slang. Then read each question and check (☑) who answers it.

	Mia	Manny	Hannah	River
1. "Well, he said that language change is inevitable, right?"	☐	☐	☐	☐
2. "Is that how everyone took it?"	☐	☐	☐	☐
3. " . . . If they can choose to change language by using slang, that means they can also choose not to use it, right?"	☐	☐	☐	☐
4. "So, isn't that a contradiction?"	☐	☐	☐	☐

B. Listen to the discussion again. Listen closely for the comments below. Check (☑) the discussion strategy the student uses.

	Agreeing	Asking for clarification or confirmation	Paraphrasing
1. **Mia:** "Yeah, OK. So what's the confusion?"	☐	☐	☐
2. **Manny:** "It's a choice, you're saying."	☐	☐	☐
3. **River:** "What he meant was that language change will happen generally."	☐	☐	☐
4. **Manny:** "But it isn't inevitable in any particular group. . . . You're right about that."	☐	☐	☐
5. **River:** "Make sense?"	☐	☐	☐

C. In small groups, discuss one or more of these topics. Try to use the discussion strategies you have learned.

- Do you think it's possible to stop—or at least slow down—language change?
- What changes have you noticed in the way language is used?
- Why do some slang terms "hang around" for years while others don't?

REVIEW *your* notes

With a partner, review your notes from the lecture. Take turns explaining the ideas from the lecture. Try to use sequence markers like those in Focus Your Attention. Then complete these notes together.

Slang

Def. of:

Who uses:

Main function of:

<u>4 Personal benefits of using:</u>

   1)

   2)

   3)

   4)

<u>3 Major inspirations for:</u>

   1)

   2)

   3)

Attitudes toward:

Now you are ready to take the Unit Test.

EXTEND *the* topic

How's your understanding of slang? Is it "the bomb"? Or is it "lame"?
Learn more slang terms and slang usage through the following listening,
reading, and research project.

A. **Listen as TV personality Jacky Giopoulos presents a brief report on IM slang. Then discuss these questions with your classmates.**

1. How many text messages do you send a day?

2. What are some of the text-based slang terms you use in speech? Are there any particularly strange ones?

B. **Do you think it is acceptable to use slang in written language, such as in school assignments, at the office, or in the press? Read the opinions of three professionals.**

Jan Dickinson, high school teacher: I've been a teacher for thirty years and not a single day has passed when I haven't heard some form of slang. I've come to realize it's part of what makes these students who they are—fine. However, I never used to see slang in students' written work—it would've been unthinkable. Today, though, slang's creeping into nearly all student writing, and it worries me. We need a standard for written language, and it's a teacher's duty to uphold that standard. Once you accept any kind of slang, you're on a slippery slope.

Sir Peter Warwick, managing director of a sportswear chain: I strongly discourage the use of slang in anything other than informal office chat, and even then I expect staff to be discriminating. For example, if I'm showing a high-level business contact around, I don't want my staff using slang in front of them. In my view, it shows a lack of professionalism, and that reflects badly on the company. In terms of written business communications, slang is never acceptable—be it e-mail or official reports. Anyone found using slang in these contexts will be quickly reprimanded.

Melanie Droghba, newspaper columnist: In my view, as the attitude toward slang has changed in recent years, so has our paper's use of it. And that's as it should be; after all, it's important that the press mirror society. I don't believe it lowers standards; rather it helps us engage and relate to ordinary people—and that's our job.

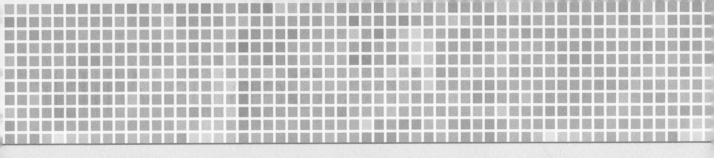

Discuss the following questions with your classmates.

1. Do you think these three views are reasonable?

2. When do you think slang is acceptable in written communication?

C. Research two slang terms.

⤑ For each term, try to find out the following information:

- the term's origins

- what the term means

- how it has disappeared and reappeared over time (where relevant)

- how its meaning has changed over time

⤑ As a class, compile your research.

⤑ Debate which terms should become "official" words in the English language.

⤑ Conclude by taking a vote on each one.

UNIT 2

The Genius Within

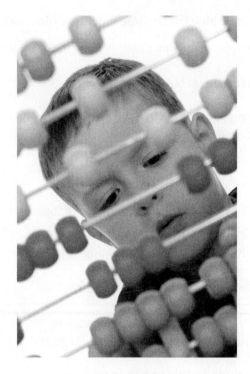

CONNECT *to the* topic

Although there is no universally agreed-upon definition of what a gifted child is, all cultures recognize that some children are special. These children seem to have a natural talent that allows them to perform in ways that are far beyond their physical age. By the age of three or four, they may have an ear for music, a talent for drawing, or a flair for performing. In other cases, their gift becomes apparent when they begin school and surprise their teachers with their understanding of mathematics, science, or literature.

Take this survey about giftedness. Check (☑) your response. Think of reasons or examples to support your opinion. Compare with a partner.

	Agree	Disagree
Many children are gifted.	____	____
I know a gifted person.	____	____
Most successful adults were gifted children.	____	____
You don't need to have natural ability to be gifted.	____	____
It's always an advantage to be gifted.	____	____

BUILD *your* vocabulary

 A. **The boldfaced words are from this unit's lecture on gifted children. Read along as you listen to each sentence. Then circle the meaning of the boldfaced word.**

1. Saki is unusually **alert** for a six-month-old baby. She seems to notice everything around her.

    a. behaving very stubbornly

    b. smiling and laughing happily

    c. watching and listening carefully

2. Zoe has an **aptitude** for sports. She learns very quickly and very well.

    a. a special quality that makes other people like her

    b. a behavior intended to make other people laugh

    c. a natural ability or skill

3. Carlos has **devoted** himself to learning how to play the cello.

    a. given a feeling of great pleasure

    b. asked strongly for something

    c. given time and perhaps money to some activity

4. Some children **exhibit** extraordinary talent at a young age.

    a. show something so that it's easy to notice

    b. get something through hard work

    c. do something to entertain people

5. Children with a good **imagination** can write interesting stories.

    a. the ability to focus on one thing intensely

    b. the ability to form creative ideas in your mind

    c. a work area that has many types of tools

6. I noticed several **inconsistencies** in his words and behavior.

    a. two or more pieces of information that do not agree with one another

    b. positive personal characteristics

    c. actions that are done to help others

7. Most children have a natural **motivation** to explore the world around them.

    a. an opinion about something

    b. an action taken to deal with a problem

    c. eagerness and willingness to do something

8. A **predominant** characteristic of most children is that they are curious about the world.

    a. more powerful than others

    b. more harmful than others

    c. more controlling than others

9. One learning **strategy** that some talented children use is to do the same activity in several different ways.

    a. a way of talking

    b. a school where students are very physically active

    c. a plan used to achieve a goal

10. Once we discover the **underlying** principles of an event, we can understand why it happens.

    a. mistaken or wrong

    b. hidden and not easy to discover

    c. strange and unexpected

B. *INTERACT WITH VOCABULARY!* **Work with a partner. Take turns saying the sentences. Notice the boldfaced words. Reorder the words to make complete sentences. Review any words you don't understand.**

1. People often (**that** / **reach** / gifted / a / is /**conclusion** / **the** / child) when that child learns extremely quickly.

2. Michelle's (dance / **aptitude** / apparent / became / for) when she was about six years old.

3. I think that (**underlying** / understand / for / the / I / **reasons**) his reluctance to join the team.

4. Some children seem to have (an / for / mathematics / **ability** / **innate** / doing).

5. Greta can write interesting stories (because / unusually / of / **imagination** / her / **creative**).

6. Miguel (has / lot **time** / **devoted** / a / of) to learning French this year.

7. Intelligent children tend to be (the / somewhat / **about** / people / **idealistic**) who they know.

8. Most intelligent children are observant; (they / many / notice / **about** / **details**) their environment.

9. As children learn how the world works, (about / can / they / **predictions** / **make**) what will probably happen next.

10. Because they encourage deeper thinking, (are / **than** / strategies / **some** / effective / **more** / **others**).

FOCUS *your* attention

EXAMPLES

Lecturers will sometimes give examples in order to illustrate a point. These examples are important because they make abstract ideas more concrete and understandable. They may also help you remember the abstract idea.

The following are some ways lecturers might present an example:

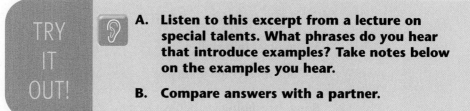

For example . . .   An example of this is . . .
For instance . . .   One example would be . . .
. . . such as . . .   Let me give you an example of this.

TRY IT OUT!

A. **Listen to this excerpt from a lecture on special talents. What phrases do you hear that introduce examples? Take notes below on the examples you hear.**

B. **Compare answers with a partner.**

Special talents

Examples:

LISTEN *to the* lecture

BEFORE YOU LISTEN

You are about to listen to this unit's lecture on gifted children. How do you think gifted children are identified?

_____

LISTEN FOR MAIN IDEAS

A. Close your book. Listen to the lecture and take notes.

B. Use your notes. Select the best answer, based on the lecture.

1. The first way gifted children are identified is that they show _____.
   a. enjoyment doing a skill
   b. interest in a skill
   c. above-average ability

2. Some psychologists believe that _____ is perhaps the best indicator of giftedness.
   a. speed of learning
   b. quality of performance
   c. number of mistakes

3. One common personality characteristic of gifted children is their _____.
   a. cheerfulness
   b. intensity
   c. verbal ability

4. Another common personality characteristic of gifted children is that they are often _____.
   a. idealistic
   b. pessimistic
   c. focused on the present

5. Gifted children often don't care about the _____ of the knowledge or skill that they are learning.

    a. difficulty

    b. usefulness

    c. popularity

6. When studying something new, gifted children are very interested in _____.

    a. telling others what they have learned

    b. the cause-and-effect relationship

    c. using their new knowledge

LISTEN FOR DETAILS

A. Close your book. Listen to the lecture again. Add details to your notes and correct any mistakes.

B. Use your notes. Decide if the statements below are *T* (true) or *F* (false), according to the lecture. Correct any false statements.

____ 1. Gifted children show strong ability in something, particularly considering their age.

____ 2. Gifted children generally make the same number of mistakes as other children.

____ 3. Many gifted children have difficulty concentrating for long periods of time.

____ 4. Most gifted children have a great deal of mental energy, but normal levels of emotional energy.

____ 5. Gifted children notice many details about the things they are interested in.

____ 6. Gifted children use their knowledge of underlying principles to make predictions.

____ 7. Gifted children generally have very good learning strategies.

TALK *about the* topic

A. Listen to the students talk about the roles of practice and innate talent in genius. Then read each opinion and check (☑) who agrees with it. More than one student may agree.

	Yhinny	Michael	May	Qiang
1. The instructor didn't emphasize the importance of innate talents enough.	☐	☐	☐	☐
2. Mozart and Emily Dickinson were naturally talented.	☐	☐	☐	☐
3. Hard work is as important as innate abilities.	☐	☐	☐	☐

B. Listen to the discussion again. Listen closely for the comments below. Check (☑) the discussion strategy the student uses.

	Offering a fact or example	Asking for clarification or confirmation	Asking for opinions or ideas
1. **Yhinny:** "You have to study something or practice something really hard for either 10,000 hours or 10 years to become really great at something."	☐	☐	☐
2. **May:** "Like talents that we're born with?"	☐	☐	☐
3. **Qiang:** "Look at Mozart and his innate talent for music . . . or Emily Dickinson and her innate talent for literature."	☐	☐	☐
4. **May:** "Mozart, he practiced for hours! His father forced him."	☐	☐	☐
5. **Michael:** "So how do I identify a gifted child?"	☐	☐	☐

C. In small groups, discuss one or more of these topics. Try to use the discussion strategies you have learned.

- Do you agree with the 10,000-hour/10-year rule of genius?
- Qiang argues that innate talent is the most important part of genius. Do you agree?
- How can people motivate themselves to practice a skill for many years?

REVIEW *your* notes

With a partner, review your notes from the lecture. Take turns explaining the ideas from the lecture, using the headings below to help you. Give examples as you discuss. Then complete these notes together.

Main points regarding gifted children

3 ways to identify	1)
	2)
	3)
3 common personality characteristics of	1)
	2)
	3)
3 Learning strategies of	1)
	2)
	3)

Now you are ready to take the Unit Test.

> **Tip!**
>
> Examples are important to write down. They make concepts more concrete and easier to understand.

EXTEND *the* topic

What have you learned about giftedness that you didn't know before? Expand that knowledge through the following listening, reading, and research project.

A. Listen to this podcast interview with Dr. Sara Andrews, who talks about problems associated with giftedness. Then discuss these questions with your classmates.

1. What would you do if you were a teacher and a student behaved in the way described in the podcast?

2. What is one other problem that parents of gifted children might face? Suggest one or two ways to deal with that problem.

B. Read this promotion of *Discover Your Genius*, a book that encourages readers to discover and develop their own genius.

Everyone has the potential for genius. The full expression of your unique genius awaits you in these pages! In *Discover Your Genius*, author Michael J. Gelb draws upon the wellspring of history's most revolutionary minds to guide you to unleash your own creativity through mental play. Gelb has assembled a "genius dream team" of ten individuals whose special "genius" characteristics you're invited to integrate into daily life.

Plato: Deepening your love of wisdom
Filippo Brunelleschi: Expanding your perspective
Christopher Columbus: Going perpendicular: strengthening your vision, optimism, and courage
Nicholas Copernicus: Reorganizing your vision of the world
Queen Elizabeth I: Wielding your power with balance and effectiveness
William Shakespeare: Cultivating your emotional intelligence
Thomas Jefferson: Celebrating your freedom in the pursuit of happiness
Charles Darwin: Developing your power of observation and cultivating an open mind
Mahatma Gandhi: Applying the principles of spiritual genius to harmonize spirit, mind, and body
Albert Einstein: Unleashing your imagination and "combinatory play"

Through reading these fascinating, accessible biographies, you can develop a personal relationship with each genius and learn how to use his or her guiding principle to enrich the quality of your life. Personal self-assessments help you gauge how each principle is working in your own life. Practical and vibrant exercises are also included to help you develop each principle fully. *Discover Your Genius* gives us the tools to improve our own mental abilities by making "genius thinking" accessible and fun!

In small groups, discuss the following questions.

1. Does this book sound appealing to you? Why or why not?

2. Which of the ten characters do you think you would have the most to learn from? Why?

3. Do you agree with the publisher's statement that "Everyone has the potential for genius"? Do you think it's possible to develop genius using Michael Gelb's method?

C. Research an adult, such as a famous athlete, musician, performer, or thinker, who you feel is gifted.

Wolfgang Amadeus Mozart, whose classical compositions have endured for more than two centuries, began composing music at the age of five.

⟶ Consider these questions:

1. Why did you choose this person?

2. At what age did the person's special ability become apparent?

3. What achievements make this person special?

4. What challenges has this person faced as a result of having special skills?

⟶ Find two pictures of the person on the Internet and use them in your presentation.

⟶ Give a five-minute presentation to the class.

UNIT 3

Social Status: Flaunting Your Success

"That look definitely says 'you.'"

CONNECT to the topic

Modern societies are often criticized for being very materialistic. In other words, people are too focused on wealth and what they own and are not concerned enough about other, more "spiritual" aspects of life. It is often argued that this trend has led to a more selfish and superficial society where people are only interested in increasing their social status.

Look at the following indicators of social status. Which do you think are the strongest? Rank them from 1 to 6, with 1 being the strongest. Compare answers with the class.

Indicator	My ranking
┄┄➤ Leisure activities (like sailing)	_____
┄┄➤ Type of car (like BMW)	_____
┄┄➤ Kind of vacations taken (like mountain climbing in Nepal)	_____
┄┄➤ Education or qualifications (like MD)	_____
┄┄➤ Job or title (like CEO)	_____
┄┄➤ Partner's appearance (fashionable, arty, etc.)	_____

BUILD *your* vocabulary

A. The boldfaced words are from this unit's lecture on social status. Listen to their definitions and fill in the blanks.

1. **advertise**: To advertise means to bring a _____ to the _____ _____ in order to encourage people to buy it.

2. **affluent**: Affluent means having _____ of _____ or _____.

3. **attaining**: Attaining means _____ or acquiring _____.

4. **consumption**: Consumption is the act of _____ and using _____.

5. **global**: Global means _____ the entire _____.

6. **hierarchies**: Hierarchies can be described as _____ that organize people into higher and _____ ranks or status.

7. **iconic**: Iconic means being _____ for _____ an important _____.

8. **income**: Income refers to the _____ a person _____ from a job.

9. **reflecting**: Reflecting means _____ or being a sign of a particular _____, _____, or feeling.

10. **status symbols**: Status symbols are the things that people do or _____ that _____ how _____ they are.

B. Study the definitions with a partner. Test each other on the definitions.

Example: A: What's a status symbol?

B: A status symbol is something that people do or own that indicates how successful they are.

C. With a partner, take five vocabulary words each and try to use them in simple sentences. Check each other's sentences. Then copy them into your notebook so that you each have a complete set of ten sentences.

D. *INTERACT WITH VOCABULARY!* Work with a partner. Cover Column A as your partner reads sentences 1–5. Listen and write the missing words in Column B. Your partner corrects your answers. Switch roles for 6–10.

Column A	Column B
1. Today, many people **concentrate on** becoming wealthier, but not necessarily better, people.	1. Today, many people **concentrate** _____ becoming wealthier, but not necessarily better, people.
2. The group came to a **consensus of opinion** on what they should wear.	2. The group came to a **consensus** _____ **opinion** on what they should wear.
3. Success usually **depends on** a mix of intelligence, hard work, and luck.	3. Success usually **depends** _____ a mix of intelligence, hard work, and luck.
4. The sales manager was awarded the annual company prize **in recognition of** his marketing success.	4. The sales manager was awarded the annual company prize **in recognition** _____ his marketing success.
5. Almost anybody can succeed in business **regardless of** his or her education.	5. Almost anybody can succeed in business **regardless** _____ his or her education.
6. Promotion is a good **indicator of** success at work.	6. Promotion is a good **indicator** _____ success at work.
7. The speaker discussed wealth as it **relates to** social status.	7. The speaker discussed wealth as it **relates** _____ social status.
8. Josh likes to **show off** his wealth by throwing lavish parties.	8. Josh likes to **show** _____ his wealth by throwing lavish parties.
9. Status can be **signified by** skills and experiences.	9. Status can be **signified** _____ skills and experiences.
10. Hard work may help you **work your way up** the career ladder.	10. Hard work may help you **work your way** _____ the career ladder.

FOCUS *your* attention

KEY TERMS AND DEFINITIONS

In a lecture, speakers will often define key terms that may be new to students and/or have a special meaning. When lecturers are focusing (or about to focus) on a key term, they often give one of these cues:

- repeat it
- spell it
- pause
- slow down
- speak more loudly
- confirm that the term was understood

- use an introductory phrase:
  There is (one key concept) . . .
  One (example) is . . .
  The first (theory) is . . .
  Let's look at (this idea of) . . .

Sometimes, a key term is followed by its definition with a verb or phrase connecting the two. Other times, the definition precedes the key term, with a verb or phrase in between. For example:

> **Prestige** <u>is</u> elevated social status.
>
> **Having prestige** <u>means</u> you'll enjoy wealth and power.
>
> **Prestige**, <u>which is</u> elevated social status, . . .
>
> Showing off your wealth, <u>called</u> **conspicuous consumption**, is . . .
>
> Buying in order to signal success, <u>referred to as</u> **conspicuous consumption**, is . . .
>
> People buy luxury goods to show their status. <u>This is what's known as</u> **conspicuous consumption**.

When noting definitions, it can be helpful to write the key term in capital letters and the definition beside or underneath it. For example:

DESIGNER CLOTHES = famous labels — e.g., Calvin Klein, Gucci; expensive; exclusive

TRY IT OUT!

A. Listen to this introduction of sociological terms. Take notes. Note the key terms and definitions you hear.

B. Compare results with a partner.

BEFORE YOU LISTEN

You are about to listen to this unit's lecture on social status. List some obvious ways and some subtle ways that people show off their social status.

Obvious: _____

Subtle: _____

LISTEN FOR MAIN IDEAS

A. Close your book. Listen to the lecture and take notes.

B. Use your notes. Decide if the statements below are *T* (true) or *F* (false), according to the lecture. Correct any false statements.

____ 1. Society decides what does and does not carry status.

____ 2. Status symbols indicate how successful we have become.

____ 3. Conspicuous consumption is about how we show off our wealth.

____ 4. Clothes no longer signal status in the twenty-first century.

____ 5. Large families have always been an indicator of higher income.

____ 6. "Storytelling" has no connection to "status skills."

LISTEN FOR DETAILS

Parents may use their children's education to give them a kind of status.

A. **Close your book. Listen to the lecture again. Add details to your notes and correct any mistakes.**

B. **Use your notes. Complete the sentences, based on the lecture.**

dancing	gardening	parents	television programs
education	impress	social class	twentieth
Europe	influence	success	wealth

1. Social status depends on things such as success, wealth, class, and _____.

2. One element of our social status we can't control is _____.

3. _____ makes people feel valued in society.

4. _____ is the quickest route to success.

5. The idea of the designer label as a status symbol originated in _____.

6. The idea of using clothes to show status originated in the _____ century.

7. Trophy kids are indicators of social status because they say something about their _____.

8. _____ are reflecting the increased interest in status skills.

9. _____ and _____ are examples of status skills.

10. Storytelling brings you status by allowing you an opportunity to _____ or _____ people with your new status skills.

TALK *about the* topic

A. Listen to the students talk about status. Then read each example and check (☑) who discusses it. More than one student may discuss it.

	Ayman	Molly	Rob	Alana
1. a designer purse	☐	☐	☐	☐
2. a family that owned a Mercedes Benz	☐	☐	☐	☐
3. a wedding with extravagant food	☐	☐	☐	☐

B. Listen to the discussion again. Listen closely for the comments below. Check (☑) the discussion strategy the student uses.

	Asking for opinions or ideas	Paraphrasing	Keeping the discussion on topic
1. **Rob:** "Hey, can we please focus on the lecture?"	☐	☐	☐
2. **Rob:** "Can anyone give some examples of some 'conspicuous consumption' that they've seen?"	☐	☐	☐
3. **Rob:** "So the car was his status symbol."	☐	☐	☐
4. **Ayman:** "So you're saying they were trying to show their guests how wealthy they were . . . "	☐	☐	☐

> **Discussion Strategy: Paraphrasing** When you paraphrase, you restate in your own words something that someone else has said or written. In the discussion, Ayman introduces a paraphrase by saying, *So you're saying . . . .* Here are some other ways of paraphrasing: *What she meant was . . . ; In other words . . .; His point was . . . ; . . . was the gist of the conversation.*

C. In small groups, discuss one or more of these topics. Try to use the discussion strategies you have learned.

- How do you feel about people using conspicuous consumption to indicate social status?
- Molly and Alana both give an example of conspicuous consumption. Can you describe an example of conspicuous consumption that you have seen?
- Why do you think some people are more interested in social status than others?

REVIEW *your* notes

With a partner, review your notes from the lecture. What key terms have you identified? Have you written any definitions? Take turns defining these key terms from the lecture. Use the key terms and definitions to reconstruct the main points of the lecture.

Definitions:

Social hierarchies -

Success and social status -

Status symbols -

Conspicuous consumption -

Designer labels -

Trophy kids -

Status skills -

Storytelling -

Now you are ready to take the Unit Test.

> **Tip!**
>
> Be sure to write down key terms. You can always look up a definition later if you missed it in class or the meaning wasn't clear.

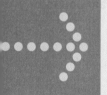

EXTEND *the* topic

Curious to learn more about status and how it shapes a life? Try the following listening, reading, and research project.

A. Listen to this trailer from a documentary exploring the link between social status and a longer life span. Then discuss these questions with some classmates. Share your answers with the class.

1. Why does Dr. Boyle talk about monkeys?

2. What might be some possible explanations for the link Dr. Boyle describes between social status and life span? The following ideas might help you:

   - the affordability of health care
   - the health risks associated with low-status lifestyles
   - education and awareness of health issues
   - the stress asociated with having less power and prestige

B. Status has traditionally come from having material success. However, there is now a new trend. Read this magazine article on one up-and-coming "status lifestyle."

Do You Dream of a Transient Lifestyle?

Here's a status lifestyle that's popular with people who want to free themselves from the hassle of possessions and permanent ownership—things like servicing and repairs, keeping in style, and theft.

"Transient lifestylers" are interested in the here and now. They typify the increasingly short satisfaction span that characterizes modern-day society. This short satisfaction span is what drives manufacturers and service organizations to continually change their products and the experiences they offer.

Transient lifestylers want quick fixes and avoid routine and boredom. How? By "collecting" as many experiences as possible and moving rapidly from one to the other. This behavior has led to them becoming known as *transumers* rather than consumers. In other words, instead of owning one expensive object, they rent, enjoy, and dispose of many different objects in order to maximize their experiences and therefore their status.

This can be expensive, though. As a result, there has been a large growth in the idea of shared ownership—of holiday apartments, private airplanes, and yachts, for example. Shared ownership allows individuals or families to share the cost of experiences that would be too costly for an individual or family to bear on their own. In this way, it can help make a transient lifestyle more affordable. Car-sharing clubs have become a particularly good example of this in recent years. People who can't afford, say, a Porsche or Aston Martin join a car-sharing club. In turn, instead of owning just one expensive car, they are able to try many different makes of exotic cars at a fraction of the cost. It's easy to see the attraction!

In pairs, briefly discuss these questions.

1. Does a transient lifestyle appeal to you? Why or why not?

2. Does it influence the way you live your life?

3. Would you say that a transient lifestyle is really less materialistic than a lifestyle based more traditionally on wealth and material possessions?

C. Research a status lifestyle.

---> Give a class presentation based on your research.

---> Choose an idea from this list, or come up with your own idea:

- eco-lifestyle

- participative lifestyle

- connecting lifestyle

---> Include the following elements:

- a description of the lifestyle you have chosen

- your opinion of the lifestyle (For example, is it appealing to you? Why or why not?)

- a statement of whether and why you believe the lifestyle is more or less materialistic than one based on wealth and material possessions

UNIT 4

The Art of Marketing in a Global Culture

CONNECT *to the* topic

Go to almost any city in the world, look around, and chances are you'll discover that much of what you see is familiar. You're likely to see familiar technology and fashions being sold in stores, worn in public, and enjoyed in homes. You'll probably run across the same Hollywood blockbusters showing at movie theaters, hear well-known music playing in nightclubs, and spot recognizable advertisements for things as mundane as laundry detergent. So although you may be thousands of miles away from home, you may feel that you can't escape the "global village" of marketing.

Think of three well-known products. Write the slogan or draw the logo associated with each product. Then survey your classmates. Keep a count of yes and no responses. Compare responses with a partner.

Product	Slogan/Logo	Have you heard of it?	Do you own/use it?	If no, do you want it?
----> _____	_____	_____	_____	_____
----> _____	_____	_____	_____	_____
----> _____	_____	_____	_____	_____

BUILD *your* vocabulary

A. The boldfaced words below are from this unit's lecture on global marketing. Listen to each sentence. Then guess the meaning of the boldfaced words. Work with a partner.

1. People's ideas about what is cool, fashionable, and desirable are starting to **converge**. Today, everybody seems to want the same products no matter where in the world they live.

2. Today's sophisticated technology **enables** business to be done at speeds and across distances not possible fifty years ago.

3. Instead of selling their **entire** product line in every country they do business in, most companies sell only some of their products in any one country.

4. Increased sales are almost **guaranteed** when marketing campaigns use celebrities. Companies pay these individuals large sums of money because they know they'll get it back through sales.

5. Many major cities around the world are becoming increasingly **homogeneous**. For instance, people dress the same, listen to similar music, admire the same sports heroes, and use similar technology.

6. Marketing campaigns have to be sensitive to **ideological** differences between cultures. Companies know, for example, that a culture's politics and social values can affect how people respond to a product.

7. Most of what we know about products, people, and places we learn through the **media** via stories, advertisements, and photographs.

8. Today, environmentally conscious leaders and businesses are trying to **promote** the idea that greener is "cooler." As a result, things like fuel-efficient cars and solar-powered houses are gaining popularity.

9. When a product has **universal** appeal, it often becomes a global success. The appeal of Coca-Cola, for example, crosses all cultural and class barriers.

10. Although it is often said that "an image is worth a thousand words," advertisements frequently use **verbal** messages to sell their products.

B. Now choose the best definition for each boldfaced word.

1. views are **converging**
   a. becoming similar
   b. becoming different
   c. remaining the same

2. **enables** business to be done
   a. makes easy
   b. makes possible
   c. makes probable

3. their **entire** product line
   a. best
   b. most popular
   c. complete

4. **guaranteed** sales
   a. unreliable
   b. certain
   c. expected

5. **homogeneous**
   a. similar
   b. varied
   c. distinctive

6. **ideological** differences
   a. based on beliefs or ideas
   b. based on logic
   c. based on economics

7. **media**
   a. TV, radio, and newspapers
   b. newscasters and reporters
   c. our everyday lives

8. **promote** the idea
   a. draw support for
   b. consider
   c. explain

9. **universal** appeal
   a. worldwide
   b. particular
   c. unique

10. **verbal** messages
   a. spoken
   b. simple
   c. clever

C. *INTERACT WITH VOCABULARY!* Work with a partner. Cover Group A as your partner reads sentences 1–4. Listen and write the missing words in Group B. Your partner corrects your answers. Switch roles for 5–8.

Group A

1. The idea of owning the latest digital device **appeals to** most young people.

2. Companies use consumers to **consult on** product image.

3. **Cooperation between** a company's head office and its local branches is essential.

4. There is always an **element of risk** with a new product.

5. Marketers place great **emphasis on** lifestyle choice.

6. Most of us are **accustomed to** seeing designer labels.

7. Shoppers are **enticed by** cheap but fashionable items.

8. Product failure is one **implication of** poor market research.

Group B

1. The idea of owning the latest digital device **appeals** _____ most young people.

2. Companies use consumers to **consult** _____ product image.

3. **Cooperation** _____ a company's head office and its local branches is essential.

4. There is always an **element** _____ **risk** with a new product.

5. Marketers place great **emphasis** _____ lifestyle choice.

6. Most of us are **accustomed** _____ seeing designer labels.

7. Shoppers are **enticed** _____ cheap but fashionable items.

8. Product failure is one **implication** _____ poor market research.

FOCUS *your* attention

SYMBOLS AND ABBREVIATIONS

Listening to a lecture can be very challenging. One useful strategy that can help you is to use symbols and abbreviations. This speeds up your note taking and helps you to keep up with the lecturer. You will often use your notes several weeks after you originally took them, so make sure all of your symbols and abbreviations are clear and easy to understand.

=	equals; is the same as	[	includes
≠	does not equal/is not the same as	]	excludes
>	is more than/larger than	+ or &	and; also
<	is less than/smaller than	. . .	continues; and so on
∴	therefore; as a result/because	$	dollars
↑	to increase	%	percent
↓	to decrease	#	number
→	leads to; causes	~	for example or approximately
←	is caused by; depends on	Δ	change
		k	thousand

ad	advertisement	fb	feedback
av	average	glob	globalization
co	company	intl	international
cult diff	cultural difference	Prof MS	Professor Michael Stevens
def	definition		
ex or e.g.	example		

TRY IT OUT!

🦻 **A.** Listen to this excerpt about e-mail marketing. Take notes using abbreviations and symbols.

B. Compare notes with a partner. Have you used similar abbreviations and symbols?

LISTEN *to the* lecture

BEFORE YOU LISTEN

You are about to listen to this unit's lecture on globalization and marketing. Globalization is the process of organizations, products, and ideas becoming international in scale and influence. Think of two causes of globalization and two consequences of globalization.

Causes: _____

_____

Consequences: _____

_____

LISTEN FOR MAIN IDEAS

A. Close your book. Listen to the lecture and take notes.

B. Use your notes. Select the best answer, based on the lecture.

1. When different cultures _____, globalization takes place.

   a. diverge   b. converge   c. expand

2. The main cause of globalization has probably been _____.

   a. flight   b. business travel   c. the entertainment industry

3. The lecturer highlights _____ as one part of the news and entertainment industry that has been a key cause of globalization.

   a. TV stars   b. advertising   c. the paparazzi

4. Politics has contributed to globalization by _____.

   a. reducing social and economic barriers   b. increasing international travel   c. helping end wars

5. Easier access to global markets _____ guarantees marketing success.

   a. usually   b. sometimes   c. never

6. "High-context" and "low-context" are ways to describe _____.

   a. business strategies b. interactive styles c. communication styles

7. Some companies wrongly assume that people with the same

   _____ will be enticed by similar products.

   a. cultural heritage b. favorite coffee c. communication style

LISTEN FOR DETAILS

A. Close your book. Listen to the lecture again. Add details to your notes and correct any mistakes.

B. Use your notes. Decide if the statements below are _T_ (true) or _F_ (false), according to the lecture. Correct any false statements.

____ 1. Globalization has created a more divided world.

____ 2. Fads and fashions are indicators of cultural differences.

____ 3. Flight has resulted in business professionals spending more time away from the office.

____ 4. Greater interaction between cultures promotes shared attitudes and values.

____ 5. Most TV programs are made with only local audiences in mind.

____ 6. Common human experiences help give TV programs international appeal.

____ 7. Fads and fashions drive advertising.

____ 8. European Union countries have cooperated successfully because their cultures are similar.

____ 9. It is the job of regional managers to ensure that a product has local appeal.

____ 10. Low-context cultures communicate less directly or explicitly than high-context cultures.

TALK *about the* topic

A. Listen to the students talk about globalization. Then read each opinion and check (☑) who agrees with it. More than one student may agree.

	Michael	Yhinny	Qiang	May
1. "We're all from different places, but we're so similar in terms of the 'stuff' that we have."	☐	☐	☐	☐
2. "Even so, we're still pretty different culturally."	☐	☐	☐	☐
3. "I think most modern societies are starting to want the same things."	☐	☐	☐	☐
4. "Hey, wouldn't it be cool to do research for a global marketing firm?"	☐	☐	☐	☐

B. Listen to the discussion again. Listen closely for the comments below. Check (☑) the discussion strategy or strategies the student uses.

	Expressing an opinion	Disagreeing	Offering a fact or example
1. **May:** "We're so similar in terms of the 'stuff' that we have."	☐	☐	☐
2. **Yhinny:** "Like, we all listen to the same musicians."	☐	☐	☐
3. **Qiang:** "Even so, we're still pretty different culturally."	☐	☐	☐
4. **Yhinny:** "I don't know. I think most modern cultures are similar, like Japan, Korea, the U.S., and the U.K."	☐	☐	☐

Discussion Strategy: Express your opinion In an academic setting, you have numerous opportunities to express your opinions—your thoughts, feelings, and positions. But while many opinions start with expressions like *I think, I believe,* and *In my opinion,* only the interesting ones continue with facts, experiences, and other forms of support!

C. In small groups, discuss one or more of these topics. Try to use the discussion strategies you have learned.

- Do you like the idea of "homogenization"? Why or why not?
- Can you think of a universal icon that has local appeal for your own culture? Try to explain its appeal.
- What kind of information do you think a researcher for a global marketing firm would try to collect?

REVIEW *your* notes

Look at your notes. Do they include any abbreviations or symbols? If so, do you remember what they mean? Reconstruct the lecture by completing the outline below, using symbols and abbreviations where appropriate. Then deliver the lecture to a classmate.

1. Definition of globalization: _____ _____

2. Indicators of cultural convergence:

   _____   _____

   _____   _____

   Ex.'s of global phenomena (e.g., cyber cafes):

   _____ _____ _____

   _____ _____ _____

3. Causes of globalization:

   i. _____   Reasons: _____
   _____

   ii. _____   Reasons: _____
   _____

   iii. _____   Reasons: _____
   _____

4. Implications of globalization for marketing:

   i. _____   Explanation: _____
   _____

   ii. _____   Explanation: _____
   _____

   Examples: _____
   _____

TAKE THE UNIT TEST

Now you are ready to take the Unit Test.

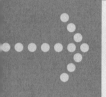

EXTEND *the* topic

Marketers often know more about you than you realize. See how in the following listening, reading, and research project.

 A. **Listen as a marketing researcher is interviewed by a business magazine correspondent about the influence of culture on purchasing decisions. Then discuss these questions with your classmates.**

1. Think of an advertisement with a promotional message and one with a preventative message. Which do you respond to better when you view it quickly?

2. What types of products are most effectively advertised using (a) promotional messages and (b) preventative messages?

B. **Many attempts have been made to describe and distinguish the behavior of different cultures. These descriptions have been used in the business world to help improve intercultural communication. Read about four ways of describing cultural behavior.**

Individualism vs. Collectivism—Individualism is found in societies that highly value individual rights and independence. In contrast, collectivism is when a society highly values the group, and everyone takes responsibility for each other.

Masculinity vs. Femininity—In masculine cultures, competitiveness, assertiveness, ambition, and the accumulation of wealth and material possessions are important. Feminine cultures, on the other hand, put more value on relationships and quality of life.

Uncertainty Avoidance—Societies concerned with uncertainty avoidance try to minimize uncertainty and insecurity. They prefer rules (for example, about religion and food) and more structured circumstances.

High/Low Power Distance Levels—In societies with high power distance levels, the most powerful members of society have a great deal more power than the least powerful members of society. In contrast, in societies with low power distance levels, there is less of a gap (or distance) between the most powerful and the least powerful members of society. This usually results in more equal rights among all members of society.

In pairs, discuss these questions.

1. How would you describe your own country in terms of these four ideas? For example, is it more individual or collective? Does it have a high or low power distance level?

2. Take one of the above ideas. In what ways (good and bad) might it affect an intercultural business discussion?

C. Choose an advertisement used in your country to sell a product that has become a global hit.

---> If possible, record or photocopy the advertisement.

---> Present it to the class.

---> Then take three to five minutes to present your ideas.

---> Think about the following:

- How does the advertisement appeal to its audience? For example, does it shock or surprise? Does it use humor, a well-known personality, clever technology, or a famous piece of music?

- Does the advertisement try to appeal to your culture in particular? In other words, does the ad's creator seem to be aware of behaviors and characteristics (such as those discussed in Part B) unique to your culture? In what ways?

- Can you think of a culture in which the advertisement might not work so well? If so, why not?

UNIT 5

Memory

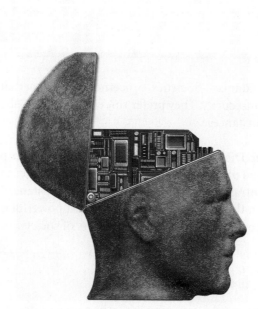

CONNECT *to the* topic

In many ways, we are our memories. When we think about who we are, we think about the events we've experienced, the people we've known, the places where we've lived and visited, as well as our ideas and feelings about a great many things. All of this is stored in our memory system. The mysteries of human memory have intrigued people for thousands of years. However, only in the past few decades have researchers begun to understand why some moments in our lives become etched in our memories forever while others evaporate almost immediately.

Read these statements about memory. Check (☑) the box that best describes you.

	Never	Sometimes	Usually	Always
⟶ I can easily remember what I did yesterday.	☐	☐	☐	☐
⟶ I can easily remember conversations I had a month ago.	☐	☐	☐	☐
⟶ I can easily recall the faces of people I met years ago.	☐	☐	☐	☐
⟶ I can remember something better if I talk about it.	☐	☐	☐	☐
⟶ I can remember things that I'm interested in.	☐	☐	☐	☐
⟶ I can remember something if I've read it several times.	☐	☐	☐	☐

Think of reasons or examples to support your answers. Compare with a partner.

BUILD *your* vocabulary

A. The boldfaced words are from this unit's lecture on memory. Listen to each sentence. Then guess the meaning of the boldfaced words. Work with a partner.

1. **Brain chemicals** can make people feel very excited or very sad. These natural substances have an extremely strong influence on our feelings.

2. Many of our memories, such as the facts and ideas that we learn in school, are **conscious**. We can recall them and explain them to others.

3. In the past **decade**, researchers have learned many new things about how memory works. And even more progress is expected in the next ten years.

4. Some of our knowledge about how to do things, such as riding a bicycle, is mostly **implicit**. We can ride the bicycle, but it's very difficult to tell another person how to do it.

5. We often think about **logical** relationships when studying something. For instance, what is the reasonable cause of something, or what will be the likely result of some event?

6. When we do mathematics, we **manipulate** information in one part of our memory system by adding, subtracting, or changing the numbers.

7. Some **psychologists** have studied the types of memory we have and how to improve memory. Thanks to this specialized study of the mind, we now know much more about memory than we did a generation ago.

8. When we feel strong emotions, our brains **release** substances. These substances go to specific parts of our brain and help us remember that event.

9. The most important function of our memory system is that it can **retain** information for long periods of time. Because of this, we can remember events that happened many years ago.

10. Some memories are stored only **temporarily**. They can be recalled very briefly, and then they fade away.

B. Now match each word to the correct definition.

____ 1. to handle, control, or move something   a. brain chemicals

____ 2. understood, but not stated directly   b. conscious

____ 3. something we notice or are aware of   c. decade

____ 4. reasonable and sensible   d. implicit

____ 5. to keep facts in your memory   e. logical

____ 6. substances that influence our thoughts and emotions   f. manipulate

    g. psychologists

____ 7. for a short time   h. release

____ 8. people who study how the mind works

    i. retain

____ 9. to let something go

    j. temporarily

____ 10. ten years

C. Say each word to yourself. Write *N* if it is a noun, *V* if it is a verb, *A* if it is an adjective, and *AV* if it is an adverb. Then use the word in a sentence.

___	1. brain chemicals	___	6. manipulate
___	2. conscious	___	7. psychologists
___	3. decade	___	8. release
___	4. implicit	___	9. retain
___	5. logical	___	10. temporarily

D. **INTERACT WITH VOCABULARY!** Work with a partner. Take turns completing each sentence with the correct form of the word. Notice the boldfaced words. Read the completed sentences aloud. Review any words you don't understand.

conscious	consciously	consciousness

1. Some of the information in our memory is _____ **available to** us.

2. Some memory enhancement techniques are **concerned with** making a _____ **effort** to relate ideas to one another.

imply	implicit	implicitly

3. Mika _____ **agreed with** Jonas by smiling at him and nodding her head.

4. The fact that information in our mind can be **stored for** different amounts of time **seems to** _____ that we have different memory systems.

logic	logical	logically

5. Our memory system is absolutely **crucial for** _____ **thought**.

6. Understanding **relationships between** ideas requires **the use of** _____ .

manipulate	manipulative	manipulation

7. When we _____ **ideas** in our minds, we can sometimes **come up with** new ways of thinking about issues.

8. Jessie's _____ **of** the information in the textbook allowed him to remember it longer.

FOCUS *your* attention

CAUSE-AND-EFFECT RELATIONSHIPS

Academic lectures often include information about cause-and-effect relationships. These relationships are very important because they clarify how different aspects of a topic relate to one another. Understanding cause-and-effect relationships will help you remember the information in the lecture.

Here are some ways lecturers might express a cause-and-effect relationship:

> **If** you hear something, **then** your auditory memory will be activated.
>
> You remember this theory **because** we talked about it for almost an hour.
>
> **Because of** his research, our understanding of memory is clearer.
>
> Using more senses **causes** us to remember more.
>
> Emotion **affects** how well we remember events.
>
> **The effect of** repeating information is better recall.
>
> Better memory **results in** more learning.

TRY
IT
OUT!

A. Listen to this excerpt from a lecture on caffeine and memory. What phrases do you hear that express a cause-and-effect relationship? Note below what causes and effects the speaker mentions.

B. Compare answers and notes with a partner.

cause	→	effect

LISTEN *to the* lecture

You are about to listen to this unit's lecture on memory. List three strategies that you use to remember information better.

_____

_____

_____

LISTEN FOR MAIN IDEAS

A. Close your book. Listen to the lecture and take notes.

B. Use your notes. Complete the main ideas, based on the lecture.

affective strategies	hold	meaningful	store
cognitive strategies	implicit	recall	unconscious
consciously available	initial moment	retain	
emotional	manipulate	senses	

1. A simple definition of memory is the ability to _____, _____, and _____ information.

2. Sensory memory concerns the _____ that we perceive something with our _____.

3. Working memory is where we temporarily _____ and _____ information.

4. Long-term memories are information that was initially processed in working memory in _____ and possibly _____ ways.

5. Declarative memory is all of the information that is _____ to us.

6. Procedural memories are _____ and _____.

7. _____ are concerned with thinking in more effective ways.

8. _____ are concerned with controlling our emotional responses.

LISTEN FOR DETAILS

A. **Close your book. Listen to the lecture again. Add details to your notes and correct any mistakes.**

B. **Use your notes. Choose the phrase that best completes each idea, based on the lecture.**

1. Sensory memory lasts approximately _____.

   a. 1–5 milliseconds   b. 10–50 milliseconds   c. 100–500 milliseconds

2. The way to record an experience in more ways in our brain is to _____.

   a. repeat the experience   b. talk about the experience   c. use multiple senses

3. The type of memory that is crucial for adding numbers or understanding logical relationships is _____.

   a. sensory memory   b. working memory   c. long-term memory

4. Long-term memory lasts from thirty seconds to _____.

   a. several days   b. several months   c. your entire lifetime

5. Riding a bicycle and playing a musical instrument are examples of _____.

   a. working memory   b. procedural memory   c. declarative memory

6. _____ concern(s) talking about information in ways that are personally meaningful.

   a. Declarative memory   b. Verbal elaboration   c. Affective strategies

7. Emotions affect memory formation because they cause _____.

   a. the release of brain chemicals   b. the release of hormones   c. the use of better affective strategies

8. A secondary benefit of using affective strategies is that they can increase a person's sense of _____.

   a. fun and challenge   b. progress and learning   c. variety

TALK *about the* topic

A. Listen to the students talk about memory. Read each question. Then check (☑) who answers it.

	Rob	Alana	Ayman	Molly
1. "Does anyone think that any of these memorization strategies actually work?"	☐	☐	☐	☐
2. "What did he call it?"	☐	☐	☐	☐
3. "Isn't that kind of common sense?"	☐	☐	☐	☐
4. "Do any of you think that you can actually change your feelings about a subject?"	☐	☐	☐	☐

Rob

Alana

Ayman

Molly

B. Listen to the discussion again. Listen closely for the comments below. Check (☑) the discussion strategy the student uses.

	Expressing an opinion	Offering a fact or example	Keeping the discussion on topic
1. **Rob:** "So why don't we start by going over some of the memorization strategies."	☐	☐	☐
2. **Rob:** "What about the affective strategy that he mentioned . . . ?"	☐	☐	☐
3. **Ayman:** "The professor is so dry."	☐	☐	☐
4. **Molly:** "We started meeting every Sunday at Café Roma to study, and we'd have questions prepared . . ."	☐	☐	☐

Discussion Strategy: Keeping the discussion on topic In study groups or other organized conversations, keeping the discussion on topic is in everyone's best interest. While tangents (related topics) can be interesting, it's fair to remind others of the focus. Common expressions include *I'd like to get back to . . .*, *We're getting a little off track . . .*, and the very informal *Anyway!*

C. In small groups, discuss one or more of these topics. Try to use the discussion strategies you have learned.

- Do you agree that memorization can be an effective approach to learning?
- Can you think of other ways to make a class more interesting?

REVIEW *your* notes

Read your notes. Work with a partner. Take turns explaining the ideas from the lecture, using the following headings to help you. Give examples or add comments as you discuss. Then complete these notes together.

- 3 main types of memory systems:
  1)

  2)

  3)

- Differences between declarative and procedural memory:

- Def. of cognitive strategies:

  Ex.:

- Def. of affective strategies:

  Ex.:

TAKE THE UNIT TEST

Now you are ready to take the Unit Test.

Tip!

Try to mark cause-and-effect relationships in your notes. This will help you understand how different ideas or processes are related.

EXTEND *the* topic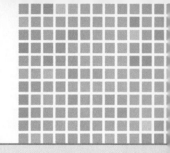

Think about this statement: "We are our memories." Do you remember where you first read or heard that statement? To build on what you've already learned, try the following listening, reading, and research project.

A. **Listen as radio journalist Marshall Duff interviews Aisha Walters, a cognitive psychologist, about the future of memory. Then discuss these questions with your classmates.**

1. Do you agree with the idea that our memory extends beyond our mind and also exists in our environment? Why or why not?

2. How does technology influence your ability to obtain and recall information? Consider devices such as computers, PDAs, and cell phones as well as computer software and the Internet.

B. **Read this newspaper article about a man suffering from amnesia (memory loss). Then answer the questions that follow.**

Mystery of the silent, talented piano player who lives for his music

Dripping wet and deeply disturbed, the "piano man" was found on the Isle of Sheppey last month. He wore a black jacket, smart trousers, and a tie, all dripping wet. Police officers tried to find out who he was but the man remained silent, unable to say who he was or where he had come from. They dried him off as best they could and took him to the emergency room at the Medway Maritime Hospital.

It was only when someone in the hospital left him with a piece of paper and pencils that the first intriguing clue about the stranger's past emerged. He drew a detailed sketch of a grand piano. Excited, hospital staff showed him into a room with a piano and he began to skillfully perform meandering, melancholy airs. The doctors were amazed at the transformation. For the first time since he had been found on Sheppey, he appeared calm and relaxed. Several weeks later he has still not spoken a word, expressing himself only through his music and often playing the piano for three or four hours until he is forcibly removed.

Do you know this man?

Some who have heard the "piano man," as he has been nicknamed, believe he may be a professional musician and may even have been performing not long before he was found—hence his smart black clothes. One theory is that he has suffered a trauma leading to amnesia, one of the methods the mind uses to retreat from a shock. Personal memories can be lost while the ability to communicate—or, for instance, play the piano—is not.

Until he is identified, the piano man will no doubt continue to play his sad but soothing music to the pleasure of those caring for him and his fellow patients.

In groups, discuss these questions.

1. What do you think happened to the "piano man"?

2. Think of five adjectives that describe how you think he might feel.

3. Share with your group an experience of amnesia you've had. For example, maybe you forgot an event in your life and the memory of it only gradually came back to you.

C.   Research a technique designed to improve memory performance.

⤏ Choose a technique.

- distributed practice
- mnemonics
- the Roman Room method
- the Journey System
- mind maps
- your own idea

⤏ Consider the following questions.

- What are the strengths and weaknesses of the approach?
- Why do you believe the technique is effective?
- Would you use the technique for important situations? Why or why not?
- How might you alter the technique to make it more effective?

⤏ Prepare a three-minute presentation in which you explain the technique to the class.

UNIT 6

The Science of Love

CONNECT *to the* topic

Throughout recorded history, one topic has attracted generation after generation of artists, musicians, and writers: love. Even today, love is seen by many people as a mysterious, uncontrollable force that can never be fully understood. However, this is exactly what researchers in many academic fields have been trying to do over the past forty years. While some people would say that these researchers have made great progress explaining the cognitive and emotional makeup of love, others would say that love should forever remain mysterious and inexplicable.

Take this survey about love. Check (☑) your opinion.

	Agree	Disagree
┈┈⟩ Love is the strongest emotion.	____	____
┈┈⟩ Love is the same in all cultures.	____	____
┈┈⟩ There are many kinds of love.	____	____
┈┈⟩ People who are in love don't behave rationally.	____	____
┈┈⟩ Love develops in a predictable way.	____	____
┈┈⟩ Love can never be explained by science.	____	____

Think of reasons or examples to support your opinion. Compare with a partner.

B U I L D *your* vocabulary

A. The boldfaced words are from this unit's lecture on love. Listen to their definitions and fill in the blanks.

1. **anthropologists**: Anthropologists study _____,
   their _____, and their _____.

2. **attachment**: Having an attachment to someone or something means that you
   feel strong _____, _____, or
   _____ toward that person or thing.

3. **characteristic**: A special _____ or _____ that
   someone or something has.

4. **emotion**: An emotion is a _____ _____
   _____ such as love or hate.

5. **enhance**: If you enhance something, you _____
   _____ _____.

6. **hormone**: A hormone is a substance in our body that influences our
   _____, _____, and _____.

7. **invoke**: If something invokes a feeling, it _____ that feeling
   _____.

8. **mutual**: This is a feeling or action that is _____ or
   _____ by two or more people toward _____
   _____.

9. **prospective**: Prospective means that a person is _____ to
   _____ a particular thing or that the event is
   _____ _____ _____.

10. **romantic**: Romantic people express strong feelings of _____
    in their _____ and _____.

B. Work with a partner. Study the definitions, and then test your partner.

   Example: A: What are anthropologists?

   B: Anthropologists study people, their societies, and their beliefs.

C. Now take five words each and try to use them in a simple sentence—one sentence for each word. Check each other's sentences, and then copy them so that you have a complete set of ten sentences each.

1. **anthropologists**:

2. **attachment**:

3. **characteristic**:

4. **emotion**:

5. **enhance**:

6. **hormone**:

7. **invoke**:

8. **mutual**:

9. **prospective**:

10. **romantic**:

D. *INTERACT WITH VOCABULARY!* Work with a partner. Take turns saying the sentences. Notice the boldfaced words. Reorder the words to make complete sentences. Review any words you don't understand.

1. Some anthropologists claim that (love / romantic / **of** / **notion** / the) is in nearly every culture.

2. Most scientists believe that (**basis** / there / **is** / **for** / a / biological) feelings of love.

3. One characteristic of people who are in love (is / **attached** / that / are / **to** / they) the object of their love.

4. Romantic people (to / the / person / **express** / their / often / **emotions**) they like.

5. People must (love / **symbols** / any / with / careful / **of** / be) that they receive.

6. Our brain (**flooded** / many / chemicals / **by** / is) when we fall in love.

7. Specific hormones and chemicals (**in** / **dominant** / **of** / each / are / **phase**) love.

8. Brain chemicals can (**of** / **feelings** / attraction / mutual / **enhance**) between two people.

9. Our body develops (**a** / **to** / hormones / some / **tolerance**) over time.

10. There is (the / some / **resistance** / idea / that / **to**) love is determined by brain chemistry.

FOCUS *your* attention

LISTS

Lecturers will sometimes give information in the form of a list. For instance, this could be lists of causes, effects, characteristics, or types of something. These lists are important because they often concern key information in the lecture; thus, this information needs to be a part of your notes if you are to understand the lecture completely and accurately. When adding a list to your notes, be sure to number each item on the list (e.g., *1, 2, 3*, etc.).

The following are some ways lecturers might indicate that they are going to list something:

> Scientists have identified **three causes for** . . .
>
> There are **four important effects of** . . .
>
> I would next like to discuss the **three major characteristics of** . . .
>
> We currently believe that there are **four types of** . . .

TRY IT OUT!

A. **Listen to this excerpt from a lecture on three kinds of love. List each kind of love along with its definition. Number each type.**

B. **Compare notes with a partner.**

3 Kinds of love	Definition
1.	

LISTEN *to the* lecture

BEFORE YOU LISTEN

You are about to listen to this unit's lecture on the scientific basis of love. The lecturer uses these terms: *romantic, biological, intensity, ritual, objects, symbol, emotional,* and *chemicals*. Think of two sentences she might say, using some of these words.

_____

_____

LISTEN FOR MAIN IDEAS

A. Close your book. Listen to the lecture and take notes.

B. Use your notes. Decide if the statements below are *T* (true) or *F* (false), according to the lecture. Correct any false statements.

____ 1. Romantic love has been identified in about half of the world's cultures.

____ 2. Face-to-face contact is an optional part of many rituals.

____ 3. Rituals cause people to focus on a common object or activity.

____ 4. Rituals promote a mutual emotion among the participants.

____ 5. Symbols are an important part of rituals.

____ 6. Testosterone and estrogen are important in the initial phase of love.

____ 7. In the second phase of love, amphetamines cause feelings of pleasure and excitement.

____ 8. In the final phase of love, few brain chemicals are secreted.

LISTEN FOR DETAILS

A. **Close your book. Listen to the lecture again. Add details to your notes and correct any mistakes.**

B. **Use your notes. Complete the sentences, based on the lecture.**

amphetamines	dopamine	heart-shaped object	PEA	testosterone
biologically based	endorphins	oxytocin	ritual	

1. Romantic love is partially _____.

2. A prescribed form of conducting a formal ceremony is a(n) _____.

3. One common symbol of love is a(n) _____.

4. _____ is a hormone that makes people alert to the presence of possible partners.

5. _____ are stimulants that make people feel alert.

6. _____ increases the heart rate and makes people more talkative.

7. _____ is a neurotransmitter that makes people feel euphoric.

Which phase of love is this couple probably in?

8. _____ make people feel a sense of security and calm.

9. _____ is known as the "cuddle chemical" because it produces feelings of attachment to another person.

TALK *about the* topic

A. Listen to the students talk about love. Read each opinion. Then check (☑) who agrees with it. More than one student may agree.

River

Hannah

	River	Hannah	Mia	Manny
1. Love is the result of a biochemical process.	☐	☐	☐	☐
2. Love isn't completely chemical or hormonal.	☐	☐	☐	☐
3. We can consciously control our feelings.	☐	☐	☐	☐

B. Listen to the discussion again. Listen closely for the comments below. Check (☑) the discussion strategy the student uses.

Mia

Manny

	Asking for opinions or ideas	Disagreeing	Trying to reach a consensus
1. **Hannah:** "Who agrees with the idea that love is the result of a biochemical process?"	☐	☐	☐
2. **River:** "Actually, I don't do much seeking. I'm usually the one being sought."	☐	☐	☐
3. **Mia:** "I don't think she was saying that."	☐	☐	☐
4. **Hannah:** "Can we at least agree that we do have some control?"	☐	☐	☐

> **Discussion Strategy: Asking for opinions or ideas** By asking for opinions or ideas, you'll not only help others become involved in the discussion, but also enrich the discussion itself. It's as easy as asking, *What do you think?* The next step—listening—is where your learning begins!

C. In small groups, discuss one or more of these topics. Try to use the discussion strategies you have learned.

- Mia strongly believes that love is the result of biochemical reactions. Do you agree?
- Manny describes his brother and his wife as "happy and content." Is this the highest goal that couples in long-term relationships can aspire to?
- Do you agree with Hannah's belief that people can control their feelings?

Read your notes. Work with a partner. Take turns explaining the ideas from the lecture, using the following headings to help you. Then complete these notes together. Be sure the items listed below are numbered in your notes.

<u>4 Characteristics of a ritual</u>

  1)

  2)

  3)

  4)

<u>3 Biochemical phases of love</u>

  1)

  2)

  3)

Now you are ready to take the Unit Test.

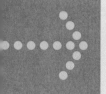 # EXTEND *the* topic

Are you head over heels for this topic? If so, learn more about romantic love in the following listening, reading, and research project.

A. Listen as author Alejandro Sanchez gives a reading from his new book about men's and women's attitudes toward romance at the Tattered Pages Bookstore. Then discuss these questions with your classmates.

1. Do you agree that men and women approach romantic relationships differently?

2. Are gender differences caused by nature, nurture, or some combination of the two?

B. In the lecture for this unit you learned that some researchers believe that love is partly based on brain chemistry and hormones. Read these short extracts of three additional explanations of why people fall in love.

Jana Spangler, psychologist: One reason why we're attracted to others is because our perceptions of beauty are partially based on physical symmetry. The more symmetrical a person's face or body, the more beautiful they appear. This is because physical symmetry is interpreted as a sign of good health and good genes. Some plastic surgeons create faces with more symmetry, using what is known as the "golden ratio" of 1:1.618. For example, the ideal ratio between the width of a person's nose and the width of their mouth is 1:1.618.

Paul Gobel, biologist: Love is partly based on smell. Although we may not be aware of it, we prefer partners who have immune systems that are different from our own, and the way that we judge another person's immune system is by the way they smell. Why would immune systems be related to attraction? Simple: When people with different immune systems have children, the children will be able to fight off a wider range of infections, so the children will probably be stronger and healthier.

Margie Lao, marriage counselor: All of us have what's called a psychological blueprint, which is the sum of our experiences and the ways they've shaped our personality. To some degree we're looking for a partner who complements our own psychological blueprint. Although we tend to like people who have similar experiences, we also look for someone who has learned to deal with life using strategies that are different from our own. This is why we say "opposites attract."

Discuss the following questions with your classmates.

1. Which of the three views do you think are reasonable?

2. In your opinion, what are other reasons that people fall in love?

C. Love is the topic of many classic films and novels.

----> As a class or in small groups, choose a film or novel from the list below or suggest your own.

Classic and popular romances (films/novels)

The Awakening
  by Kate Chopin

The Bridges of Madison County
  by Robert James Waller

Casablanca

City Lights (with Charlie Chaplin)

Doctor Zhivago

The English Patient
  by Michael Ondaatje

Madame Bovary
  by Gustave Flaubert

Pride and Prejudice
  by Jane Austen

The Scarlet Letter
  by Nathaniel Hawthorne

Sleepless in Seattle

When Harry Met Sally

While You Were Sleeping

----> Discuss the film or novel, using the chart to discuss how it relates to your own culture.

In the film/novel . . .	In your culture . . .
How does the couple meet?	How do people in search of romantic love meet?
What phases of love does the film/novel depict?	How do popular films/novels in your culture depict the phases of love?
Why is the couple attracted to one another?	What do people do to attract others?
What does the couple say or do that makes them appear to be in love?	How do couples in love behave?
Will it last? Why?	Who do you know with a long-lasting relationship? What's their "secret"?

UNIT 7

Mission to Mars

CONNECT *to the* topic

The first and last time humankind visited another world was in 1969 when two astronauts stepped onto the Moon. The world watched the event in wonder, and many people expected trips to planets to follow. But that hasn't happened. The fact is, even Mars, our nearest planetary neighbor, is five times farther from Earth than the Moon. And that presents enormous technical challenges despite huge advances over the past forty years. Can we expect to see astronauts exploring the Martian world in the near future? It's unlikely. Most experts believe we'll have to wait at least another twenty years.

Humans' desire to explore the universe is perhaps stronger today than at any time in history. In small groups, list some of the advantages and disadvantages of space exploration. As a class, discuss your results.

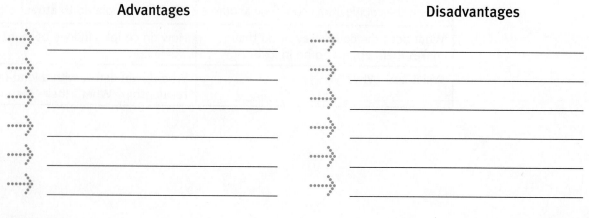

Advantages	Disadvantages

BUILD *your* vocabulary

A. The boldfaced words are from this unit's lecture on Mars. Listen to each sentence. Then guess the meaning of the boldfaced words. Work with a partner.

1. All large projects have to meet **bureaucratic** requirements. They have to get approval from different individuals, departments, or organizations.

2. Scientists spend thousands of hours first **detecting** then solving potential problems before any spacecraft is given the all-clear for takeoff.

3. High levels of mental fitness and physical training are **essential** for all astronauts. Without them, astronauts would be unable to do their job.

4. As the largest space researcher in the world, NASA has **facilities** located in more than a dozen cities across the United States.

5. Astronauts are trained to **maintain** their composure in situations that are dangerous and stressful. They must never panic.

6. Some believe that money spent on the space program should be used instead to help **overcome** problems on Earth. We should first solve things like global warming and world hunger, they say.

7. NASA has invested billions of dollars of **resources**—both human and technological—in its space program.

8. Politicians often argue that NASA's space research is not **sustainable** because the cost of development programs is so high. They say there's not enough money to keep the program going.

9. Despite cutting-edge technology, spacecrafts are still notoriously **unreliable**. Their performance in space can't be trusted.

10. Scientists have already produced and successfully tested a **vehicle** for traveling across the Martian surface. It looks like a fancy off-road truck but moves more slowly.

B. Now choose the best definition for each boldfaced word.

1. **bureaucratic** requirements

   a. technical
   b. health
   c. official

2. **maintain** composure

   a. build
   b. enjoy
   c. keep

3. **detecting** problems

   a. creating
   b. locating
   c. searching for

4. **essential**

   a. important
   b. difficult
   c. absolutely necessary

5. **facilities**

    a. houses
    b. buildings
       and equipment
    c. universities

6. **overcome** problems

    a. create
    b. fix
    c. move past

7. to invest in **resources**

    a. ideas
    b. sources of supply
       or support
    c. technology

8. research is **sustainable**

    a. can continue
    b. desirable
    c. adequate

9. spacecrafts are **unreliable**

    a. undependable
    b. loud
    c. unsophisticated

10. a **vehicle**

    a. form of transport
    b. piece of scientific
       equipment
    c. type of camera

C. *INTERACT WITH VOCABULARY!* **Work with a partner. Cover Group A as your partner reads sentences 1—3. Listen and write the missing words in Group B. Your partner corrects your answers. Switch roles for 4–6.**

Group A

1. Biofuel is an **alternative to** regular gasoline.

2. Psychologists are **concerned about** the dangers of space travel.

3. Professor Alvarez is a **contender for** the Nobel Prize.

4. Despite the dangers of space travel, people's enthusiasm has not **gone away**.

5. Scientists realize that there are many **obstacles to** a successful Martian mission.

6. Scientists are trying to meet the technological **challenge of** extended space travel.

Group B

1. Biofuel is an **alternative** _____ regular gasoline.

2. Psychologists are **concerned** _____ the dangers of space travel.

3. Professor Alvarez is a **contender** _____ the Nobel Prize.

4. Despite the dangers of space travel, people's enthusiasm has

    not **gone** _____.

5. Scientists realize that there are many **obstacles** _____ a successful

    Martian mission.

6. Scientists are trying to meet the technological **challenge** _____ extended

    space travel.

FOCUS *your* attention

ORGANIZATION

Good notes are well-organized notes.

- They should be arranged neatly and logically.
- They should give you an at-a-glance "picture" of the structure of the lecture.
- They should enable you to recall the content of the lecture at a later date.

One effective way of organizing your notes is to write the main ideas on the left side of your page and the more detailed, supporting ideas on the right side. There may be a number of different levels of detail, so as your notes move to the right, the level of detail increases. Your notes might look like this:

[Main idea 1]

                [Supporting idea 1]

                    [Example 1]

                [Supporting idea 2]

                [Supporting idea 3]

                    [Example 1]

                    [Example 2]

[Main idea 2]

                [Supporting idea 1]

TRY IT OUT!

A. **Listen to this excerpt of a speaker discussing why space exploration may not be a good idea. Take notes. Try to organize your notes from left to right according to the main ideas and details you hear.**

B. **Compare notes with a partner. Can you improve them?**

LISTEN *to the* lecture

You are about to listen to this unit's lecture on traveling to Mars. With a partner, come up with four challenges of making such a trip.

1. _____

2. _____

3. _____

4. _____

LISTEN FOR MAIN IDEAS

A. Close your book. Listen to the lecture and take notes.

B. Use your notes. Decide if the statements below are *T* (true) or *F* (false), according to the lecture. Correct any false statements.

____ 1. The main purpose of a trip to Mars would be to find other signs of life.

____ 2. The three main obstacles to a trip to Mars are the spacecraft, supplies, and maintaining astronauts' health.

____ 3. A space capsule is the most likely form of transport for astronauts making the journey to Mars.

____ 4. The lecturer discusses three main methods of propulsion for the spacecraft.

____ 5. Scientists are unable to build a spacecraft that could carry the water, fuel, air, and food for a mission to Mars.

____ 6. The political and bureaucratic challenges of such a mission are easy to solve compared to the technical challenges.

LISTEN FOR DETAILS

A. **Close your book. Listen to the lecture again. Add details to your notes and correct any mistakes.**

B. **Use your notes. Circle the best answer, based on the lecture.**

1. _____ have developed new space programs.

   a. India and Japan   b. Korea and China   c. China and Japan

2. The space shuttle is unsuitable for a trip to the planet Mars because

   _____.

   a. it is too old   b. it is too light and unreliable   c. of its wings

3. A new _____ is being developed as part of a future International Space Station project.

   a. type of fuel   b. space capsule   c. lightweight space suit

4. A plasma propulsion rocket produces acceleration by using

   _____.

   a. magnets and gas   b. nuclearly charged gas   c. ions

5. The main disadvantage of a plasma propulsion rocket is _____.

   a. cost   b. the time needed to develop it   c. harm to the environment

6. A spacecraft couldn't carry the water, fuel, air, and food required for a mission to Mars because of _____.

   a. room   b. weight   c. radiation concerns

7. A round trip to Mars would take _____.

   a. fourteen months   b. one year and four months   c. forty months

8. Water manufactured on Mars could be used for drinking and producing _____.

   a. oxygen   b. medicines   c. food and fuel

TALK *about the* topic

A. Listen to the students talk about interplanetary travel. Read each opinion. Then check (☑) who disagrees. More than one student may disagree.

	Alana	Ayman	Molly	Rob
1. Earth is going to be uninhabitable someday.	☐	☐	☐	☐
2. It's fatalistic to think that pollution and war will force people to colonize other planets.	☐	☐	☐	☐
3. The lecture is simple.	☐	☐	☐	☐
4. The lecture is difficult.	☐	☐	☐	☐

B. Listen to the discussion again. Listen closely for the comments below. Check (☑) the discussion strategy or strategies the student uses.

	Expressing an opinion	Disagreeing	Keeping the discussion on topic
1. **Alana:** "You guys are a bunch of fatalists."	☐	☐	☐
2. **Alana:** "No, no. Come on."	☐	☐	☐
3. **Ayman:** "So, does anyone want to review the lecture?"	☐	☐	☐
4. **Ayman:** "No, it's not that hard. It's just basic problem solving. It's not rocket science!"	☐	☐	☐

Discussion Strategy: Expressing disagreement In most conversations, expressing disagreement without seeming too disagreeable is key! One way to do so is to first acknowledge the other person's point: *I see what you're saying, but . . .* Or you can be direct: *I simply disagree.* Some people like to soften their position with an apology: *I'm sorry, but . . .* And of course, body language and tone can further *shape* your message.

C. In small groups, discuss one or more of these topics. Try to use the discussion strategies you have learned.

- Does the idea of space exploration interest you? Why?
- Do you agree that Earth will be uninhabitable someday? How can we solve our planet's problems?
- Molly mentions overpopulation as a future problem. Do you think governments should limit family size?

REVIEW *your* notes

In Focus Your Attention, you learned to organize your notes more effectively by putting the main ideas on the left and the details on the right. With the help of your notes and the basic outline below, try to reconstruct the lecture with a partner. Add as much detail as possible.

Space travel is not just a luxury, it's a necessity:

Mars = best candidate for a space colony:

3 Main obstacles to a Martian mission:

Political and bureaucratic challenges:

Now you are ready to take the Unit Test.

> **Tip!**
>
> Remember: There are many ways to organize your notes. You can use symbols, like bullets or arrows. Or you might prefer the more formal outline style, with numbers and letters. Choose a style that suits you.

EXTEND *the* topic

Have your feelings about space exploration changed throughout this unit? How? Learn more through the following listening, reading, and research project.

A. **Listen to the audio from a blogcast interview with sociologist Michael Friege, who explains why space exploration is important. Then discuss this question in small groups.**

What do you think of the exploration of space as a response to the population pressures and environmental factors that humankind faces? Explain your answers.

B. **In the unit lecture you heard concerns about Earth's sustainability. Below are brief descriptions of four initiatives designed to reduce environmental damage to Earth. Read about the initiatives.**

Live Earth (a concert held in 2007)—This was a huge music event that brought together more than two billion people in order to raise awareness of climate change. Live Earth consisted of twenty-four hours of music across seven continents, and it marked the beginning of a multi-year mass persuasion campaign led by the Alliance for Climate Protection. The campaign's intent was to move individuals, corporations, and governments to take action to try to halt climate change.

The Kyoto Protocol (a political agreement initiated in 1997)—This was an agreement made under the United Nations Framework Convention on Climate Change. The original purpose was to get as many countries as possible to commit to reducing their emissions of carbon dioxide and five other greenhouse gases. More than 130 countries initially signed the agreement (accounting for 60 percent of emissions); however, their only obligation was to monitor and report their

emissions. The United States and Australia were two UN countries who refused to sign the agreement.

Saving Planet Earth (a TV documentary first aired in 2007)—In this series, Sir David Attenborough and the world-renowned BBC Natural History Unit explain how the destruction of crucial habitat is affecting the future of many of Earth's species. In each episode, a celebrity highlights the plight of a threatened animal, such as the orangutan or the tiger. The series concludes with a live fund-raising extravaganza raising cash for charities involved in global conservation.

An Inconvenient Truth (a documentary film released in 2006)—This award-winning film about global warming was presented by former U.S. Vice President Al Gore and earned $49 million worldwide in its first box office year. In it Gore reviews scientific opinions on climate change, discusses the politics and economics of global warming, and describes the devastating consequences if greenhouse gases are not significantly reduced in the very near future. The film ends with a statement that global warming can be reversed and a personal plea to viewers to help him in his efforts.

In groups, consider these questions.

1. Which of the initiatives do you think are most effective? Why?

2. Which do you think are least effective? Why?

3. What is an initiative you could imagine leading or becoming involved in?

C. **Research a space mission such as Cloudsat, the Phoenix Mars Mission, or NASA's Dawn Mission (more at www.jpl.nasa.gov/missions).**

⸺▷ Consider these questions.

- What is the purpose of the mission?

- What are the expected benefits?

- What technology is being used?

- What is the timescale for the mission?

- What are some of the challenges the mission faces, and what are the possible solutions (if any)?

⸺▷ Prepare a five-minute presentation to the class.

UNIT 8

Big Brother and the Surveillance Society

CONNECT *to the* topic

Civil liberties groups argue that in most modern-day societies, the lives of ordinary citizens are no longer private in the way they once were. These groups are concerned that political, commercial, and security organizations now have access to detailed information about us, ranging from our whereabouts to our financial dealings to our personal lifestyle choices. What is particularly worrying is the fact that many of us are unaware that we are being "watched" in this way.

Take this survey about security and being watched. Check (☑) your opinion. Compare responses with a partner.

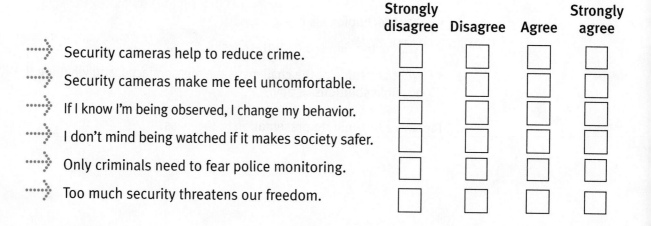

	Strongly disagree	Disagree	Agree	Strongly agree
Security cameras help to reduce crime.	☐	☐	☐	☐
Security cameras make me feel uncomfortable.	☐	☐	☐	☐
If I know I'm being observed, I change my behavior.	☐	☐	☐	☐
I don't mind being watched if it makes society safer.	☐	☐	☐	☐
Only criminals need to fear police monitoring.	☐	☐	☐	☐
Too much security threatens our freedom.	☐	☐	☐	☐

BUILD *your* vocabulary

A. The boldfaced words are from this unit's lecture on surveillance. Listen to their definitions and fill in the blanks.

1. **civil liberties**: Civil liberties are the _____ and _____ people have in society.

2. **commercial**: Commercial means having to do with _____ or _____.

3. **composite**: Composite means _____ up of _____ _____ or materials.

4. **controversial**: Something that is controversial causes a _____ of _____.

5. **deterrent**: A deterrent is a way of _____ people from _____ something.

6. **security**: Security refers to _____ taken by agencies to _____ us.

7. **sophisticated**: If something is sophisticated, it's _____ or _____.

8. **suspected**: Somebody who is suspected is _____ to be _____ for doing something _____.

9. **techniques**: Techniques are particular _____ or ways of _____ something.

10. **via**: Via means _____, by, or _____ way of— for example, "She flew from Prague to New York via London."

B. Study the definitions with a partner. Then test each other on the definitions.

Example: A: What are techniques?

B: Techniques are ways of doing something.

C. *INTERACT WITH VOCABULARY!* Work with a partner. Cover Column A as your partner reads sentences 1–5. Listen and write the missing words in Column B. Your partner corrects your answers. Switch roles for 6–10.

Column A	Column B
1. An important **aspect of** police work is the collecting of criminal evidence.	1. An important **aspect** _____ police work is the collecting of criminal evidence.
2. Criminals are carefully **monitored by** police.	2. Criminals are carefully **monitored** _____ police.
3. The boy was **suspected of** theft.	3. The boy was **suspected** _____ theft.
4. Criminals **take advantage of** new technology to commit sophisticated crimes.	4. Criminals **take advantage** _____ new technology to commit sophisticated crimes.
5. Security cameras protect us from **threats to society**.	5. Security cameras protect us from **threats** _____ **society**.
6. We frequently give organizations **access to** our personal details.	6. We frequently give organizations **access** _____ our personal details.
7. Being closely monitored can feel **equivalent to** being in prison.	7. Being closely monitored can feel **equivalent** _____ being in prison.
8. Tighter security makes it less likely that we'll be **exposed to** violence in public places.	8. Tighter security makes it less likely that we'll be **exposed** _____ violence in public places.
9. Security cameras have **become part of** normal everyday city life.	9. Security cameras have **become part** _____ normal everyday city life.
10. Many of us are **unaware of** being tracked by security cameras.	10. Many of us are **unaware** _____ being tracked by security cameras.

FOCUS *your* attention

NUMBERS AND STATISTICS

Whether you are studying humanities, social sciences, or physical sciences, you will often work with numbers and statistics. Listen carefully for stressed syllables, since many numbers sound similar but have different stress patterns (A). Also listen for number group markers such as *hundred*, *thousand*, and *million* (B). Finally, note that the word *and* can come before the tens units, although many speakers don't use it (C). For example:

(A) 13 – thir**teen**; 30 – **thir**ty

(B) 34,832 – thirty-four **thousand**, eight **hundred**
          thirty-two

      256,375 – two **hundred** fifty-six **thousand**, three
          hundred seventy-five

      18,035,699 – eighteen **million**, thirty-five **thousand**, six
          hundred ninety-nine

(C) 263 – two hundred sixty-three

TRY IT OUT!

A. **Listen to this excerpt about surveillance cameras in New York City. Note as many statistics as you can below.**

B. **Compare notes with a partner.**

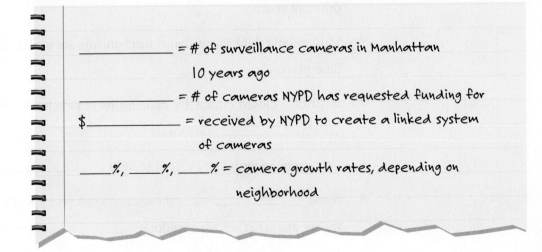

_____ = # of surveillance cameras in Manhattan
                10 years ago
_____ = # of cameras NYPD has requested funding for
$_____ = received by NYPD to create a linked system
                of cameras
____%, ____%, ____% = camera growth rates, depending on
                neighborhood

LISTEN *to the* lecture

BEFORE YOU LISTEN

You are about to listen to this unit's lecture on the increasing use of surveillance systems in the world. List four ways that information about people can be obtained as they go about their day-to-day activities.

1. _____   3. _____

2. _____   4. _____

LISTEN FOR MAIN IDEAS

A. **Close your book. Listen to the lecture and take notes.**

B. **Use your notes. Complete these main ideas, based on the lecture.**

biometric facial recognition	invasion	suspected
credit card	organizations	three hundred
government	solve crimes	watching

1. Surveillance is the act of carefully _____ a person or place, especially one that's _____.

2. Civil liberties groups are concerned about the information on individuals that the _____ and private _____ can get from different sources.

3. Most people think surveillance mechanisms are a(n) _____ of their privacy.

4. In Britain, closed-circuit TV cameras record each citizen up to _____ times a day.

5. Cell phone records can be used to help _____.

6. Some _____ transactions can provide information on where we are and what we are spending.

7. One sophisticated surveillance technique is called _____.

Increasingly, closed-circuit TV cameras can be found in public places, including food courts.

LISTEN FOR DETAILS

A. **Close your book. Listen to the lecture again. Add details to your notes and correct any mistakes.**

B. **Use your notes. Decide if the statements below are *T* (true) or *F* (false), according to the lecture. Correct any false statements.**

____ 1. Civil liberties groups completely support all uses of surveillance.

____ 2. Societies where people are monitored a lot are called intrusion cultures.

____ 3. The number of surveillance cameras in New York City has increased 15 percent in the past few years.

____ 4. Cell phones help solve crimes by allowing police to communicate with each other more quickly and easily.

____ 5. A technique called triangulation allows police to locate cell phone users.

____ 6. Biometric facial recognition has been used in airports and hospitals.

____ 7. EPIC is probably a civil liberties group.

____ 8. The lecturer generally appears to support the use of surveillance mechanisms.

TALK *about the* topic

A. Listen to the students talk about surveillance. Read each opinion. Then check (☑) who expresses it.

	May	Qiang	Yhinny	Michael
1. Not all surveillance is for our own good.	☐	☐	☐	☐
2. The lecturer exaggerated; Big Brother isn't watching over us *all* the time.	☐	☐	☐	☐
3. Cameras on public transportation are comforting.	☐	☐	☐	☐
4. Traffic cameras that capture images from people's homes and feed them to the Internet are intrusive.	☐	☐	☐	☐

B. Listen to the discussion again. Listen closely for the comments below. Check (☑) the discussion strategy the student uses.

	Agreeing	Asking for clarification or confirmation	Trying to reach a consensus
1. **Michael:** "She said not all surveillance is for our own good, right?"	☐	☐	☐
2. **Qiang:** "She says something like, 'Orwellian.' What is that?"	☐	☐	☐
3. **Michael:** "In general, we all agree that some surveillance is necessary, but not all surveillance is good?"	☐	☐	☐
4. **Yhinny:** "I would say so."	☐	☐	☐

Discussion Strategy: Reaching a consensus Getting a group to reach a consensus, or agree, can be challenging. One approach is to use questions to identify areas of agreement (*So, When is everyone free to meet again?*). You can follow by making suggestions based on feedback (*Sounds like Sunday is open for everyone—does that work?*).

C. In small groups, discuss one or more of these topics. Try to use the discussion strategies you have learned.

- What are examples of necessary and unnecessary surveillance?
- Would you prefer to live in a society that has no surveillance, and therefore possibly less security, or one that has heavy surveillance but is possibly safer?

REVIEW *your* notes

Read your notes. Did you write down any numbers or statistics? Explain them to a partner. Then try to reconstruct the lecture, using your notes and the cues below.

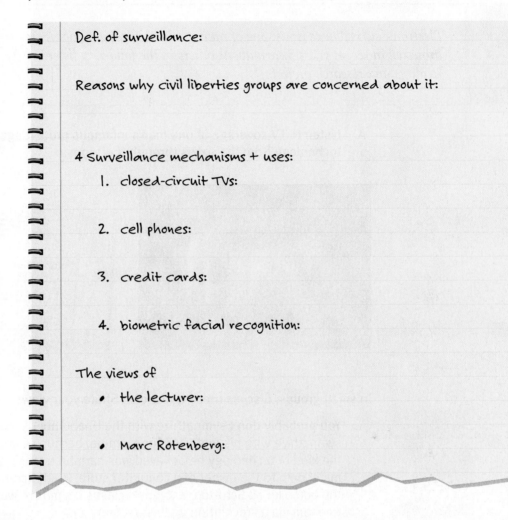

Def. of surveillance:

Reasons why civil liberties groups are concerned about it:

4 Surveillance mechanisms + uses:

1. closed-circuit TVs:

2. cell phones:

3. credit cards:

4. biometric facial recognition:

The views of

• the lecturer:

• Marc Rotenberg:

TAKE THE UNIT TEST

Now you are ready to take the Unit Test.

Tip!

Note how decimals, fractions, powers, and square roots are said.

Decimals:
4.6 – four point six
.04 – point zero/oh four

Fractions:
⅛ – one/an eighth
¼ – one/a quarter
⅓ – one/a third
½ – one/a half
⅝ – five eighths
2⅓ – two and . . .

Powers:
3^2 – three squared
12^3 – twelve to the third power
OR twelve cubed

Square roots:
$\sqrt{64}$ – the square root of sixty-four
$\sqrt{10}$ – the square root of ten

EXTEND *the* topic

Electronic surveillance is just one of many technological developments protested in recent years. Learn about others in the following listening, reading, and research project.

A. Listen to TV coverage of one man's infamous protest against modern technology from the 1970s through the 1990s.

In small groups, discuss these questions. Share your views with the class.

1. You probably don't sympathize with the Unabomber's methods, but do you sympathize with his motives? For example, because computers represented the kind of technology he believed was harmful to society, Kaczynski sent a mail bomb to the owner of a computer store, Hugh Scrutton. Upon exploding, the bomb killed Scrutton. Kaczynski claims his motive was to protect people's freedom via a "revolution against technology."

2. Do you think it's ever acceptable to use violence in order to fight for something you believe in?

B. Surveillance raises important questions about people's right to privacy. Often, the news and entertainment media are criticized for invading people's privacy in order to get a celebrity scoop or a front-page photograph. Read three views on this issue.

Karl Hart, newspaper editor: It's right that politicians and celebrities are subjected to intense media interest. Politicians are public figures—they're responsible to the people who elected them and should always be held accountable, in public or private. Same with celebrities. They're happy for the press to follow them around when they're trying to become famous. So they can't really complain when the press catches them doing something *in*famous.

Dr. Jane Rickson, ethics professor: It doesn't matter what a person's profession is, everybody has a right to a private life. They have a right to expect that what they do behind closed doors will stay there—not be displayed on some front page just to increase sales. The only time it's acceptable for private information to be made public is when it's in the public interest. For example, if a senator is publicly supporting "family values," but privately having an extramarital affair, then it should be news. Otherwise, it's invasion of privacy.

Samantha Davies, fashion model: I've had lots of run-ins with the media and even won two court cases on the basis that my privacy was invaded. I can understand the need "to get the story." And I can see that as public figures we should give something back to the fans who have made us celebrities. I think if journalists weren't so aggressive, celebrities would be more willing to cooperate with them. If they'd just ask permission and sometimes accept "no" for an answer, things would improve a lot.

In pairs, discuss these questions.

1. Which of the above views do you agree with most? Why?

2. Create privacy guidelines for the news and entertainment media to follow.

C. Choose one of the research projects below. Present a three-minute report of your findings to your classmates.

······> Identify all of the surveillance opportunities in the area around where you live, work, or go to school. Make a list of all possible sources— cameras, police outposts, cash machines, Internet cafes, etc.

······> Research a recent development in surveillance. Choose one of the following areas as the focus of your research:

- new technology
- protest by a civil liberties group
- implementation of a system by government

UNIT 9

Animal Communication

"What is it, Fluffy? You want to go outside?"

CONNECT *to the* topic

Scientists have long believed that humans can communicate a seemingly infinite number of ideas, while animals can express only rudimentary ideas. But is this actually the case? Animals appear to have far more sophisticated abilities than was once believed. Some researchers now think that in order to unravel the mysteries of animal communication, we must first answer this question: Do humans and animals communicate in the same way?

Consider whether you agree or disagree with the following statements. Check (☑) your response.

	Agree	Disagree
Animals communicate in many different ways.	____	____
Animals can understand what people are feeling.	____	____
Animals can express emotion.	____	____
Animals can use simple words.	____	____
Adult animals teach their young to communicate.	____	____
Animal communication is fundamentally the same as human communication.	____	____

Think of reasons or examples to support your opinion. Compare responses with a partner.

BUILD *your* vocabulary

A. The boldfaced words are from this unit's lecture on animal communication. Listen to each sentence. Then guess the meaning of the boldfaced words. Work with a partner.

1. Gerhard speaks English with a slight German **accent**. His pronunciation is a little different from someone who grew up in an English-speaking country.

2. Every language has many **discrete** sounds. For instance, in English, the *p* in the word *pail* and *t* in the word *tail* are pronounced in different ways.

3. Some animals make meaningful sounds that are **distinct** from one another. For example, a low-pitched sound may communicate anger and a high-pitched sound excitement.

4. Human languages are very **flexible**. People can say the same thing in many different ways.

5. The songs used by older birds are passed on to the younger **generation** of birds. In this way, the young birds learn to sing like their parents.

6. Some chimpanzees have been taught to express an **impressive** number of ideas. Most people are surprised to learn that some chimps understand several hundred words.

7. Dogs express happiness using **nonverbal behavior**. They jump up and down in an excited way and wag their tails quickly.

8. Human communication is fairly **precise**, so we usually understand each other. For example, if you say, "Look at my new hairstyle," I know where to look.

9. Almost all animal communication seems **random** when we look at grammar. Animals seem to use no clear grammar rules.

10. Although some animals can communicate well within their own species, **ultimately**, their ability to communicate with humans is quite limited.

B. Match each word to the correct definition.

a.	accent	d.	flexible	g.	nonverbal behavior	i.	random
b.	discrete	e.	generation	h.	precise	j.	ultimately
c.	distinct	f.	impressive				

_____ 1. able to change or be changed easily

_____ 2. when ideas or things are separate from each other

_____ 3. something that makes a strong impression or causes admiration

_____ 4. expressing meaning without words

_____ 5. a group of people born around the same time

_____ 6. exact

_____ 7. the way a person pronounces words

_____ 8. in the end; finally

_____ 9. existing in a way that seems to be without reason; unpredictable

_____ 10. clearly different or separate

C. **Say each word to yourself. Write _N_ if it is a noun and _A_ if it is an adjective. Then use each word in a sentence.**

_____	1. accent	_____	6. impressive
_____	2. discrete	_____	7. nonverbal behavior
_____	3. distinct	_____	8. precise
_____	4. flexible	_____	9. random
_____	5. generation	_____	10. ultimate

D. _INTERACT WITH VOCABULARY!_ **Work with a partner. Take turns saying the sentences. Notice the boldfaced words. Reorder the words to make complete sentences. Review any words you don't understand.**

1. Some people (that / **communicate** / they / believe / can **/ with**) animals.

2. Animals (**information** / sophisticated / can **convey** / **to** / another / one) using various means.

3. Some animals can express (**of** / the / **perceptions** / world / their) fairly precisely.

4. The sounds that animals make (past / **to** / not / events / **refer** / do).

5. There is (**nothing** / meaning / the / **about** / **arbitrary**) of a lion's roar.

6. Both animals and people (**of** / **range** / use / **wide** / **a**) nonverbal behavior.

7. People can produce (**number** / unlimited / sentences / an / **of**) by using the words and grammar of their language.

8. Animals do not (**capacity** / grammar / have / using / **for** / the).

9. Animal communication seems (limited / **compared** / when / very / **to**) human speech.

10. Children (the / are / **at** / acquiring / accent / **skilled**) used in their social community.

FOCUS *your* attention

COMPARISONS AND CONTRASTS

In a lecture that includes comparisons and contrasts, it is important to note how items are similar or different. The words on the top are used to indicate similarities, or comparisons. Those on the bottom indicate differences, or contrasts.

like	likewise	in a similar manner
in the same way	as with . . . so too with	both . . . and . . .
as . . . as	not only . . . but also	parallels
also	similar to / similarly	in like fashion
but	more (than)	on the other hand
however	whereas	in contrast
conversely	different from	unlike
while	less (than)	although

One way to contrast two or more items is to note the similarities and differences separately.

Kangaroo rats
- communicate by stamping their feet
- ex. "words": "This is mine!" + "Go away!"

Sparrows
- communicate by singing
- ex. "words": "Above you!" + "Be careful!"

Another way is to note each point of comparison and contrast separately.

	Kangaroo rats	Sparrows
Mode of communication	stamping their feet	singing
Example "words"	"This is my territory!"	"Be careful!"

TRY IT OUT!

A. Listen to this excerpt from a discussion on two modes of animal communication. Take notes and organize them so that the comparisons and contrasts are clear.

B. Compare notes with a partner. Can you improve them?

LISTEN *to the* lecture

BEFORE YOU LISTEN

You are about to listen to this unit's lecture on animal communication. List three ways that animals communicate.

1. _____

2. _____

3. _____

LISTEN FOR MAIN IDEAS

A. Close your book. Listen to the lecture and take notes.

B. Use your notes. Select the best answer, based on the lecture.

1. Like humans, animals use both _____ to communicate.

   a. sounds and nonverbal communication
   b. words and gestures
   c. sentences and facial expressions

2. Human communication is _____ than animal communication.

   a. older
   b. more flexible
   c. more direct

3. _____ is defined as the lack of a logical relationship between a sound and its meaning.

   a. Arbitrariness
   b. Distance
   c. Transmission

4. The ability to communicate about things that are not physically present is called _____.

   a. abstraction
   b. complexity
   c. displacement

5. Bees are able to use dances to communicate information about

   _____.

   a. their relationship with other bees
   b. the presence of enemies
   c. the location of a food source

6. The idea that language is passed from one generation to the next is called cultural _____.

   a. communication
   b. transmission
   c. displacement

7. _____ means that language is made up of separate units that can be combined in many ways.

    a. Discreteness   b. Phonology   c. Vocabulary

LISTEN FOR DETAILS

A. Close your book. Listen to the lecture again. Add details to your notes and correct any mistakes.

B. Use your notes. Complete the sentences, based on the lecture.

accents	displacement	phrases	sophistication
arbitrary	distinct meanings	scientists	sounds
discreteness	grammar		

1. The growl of an angry dog illustrates that much of animal communication is not _____.

2. Meerkats are unusual animals because they are able to use about twenty sounds that have _____.

3. Human languages are very flexible because they are made up of a wide range of _____.

4. That dogs only express dislike of cats when a cat is present indicates that dogs do not have the capacity for _____.

5. The meaning of bee dances is so precise that even _____ can understand where the food is located.

6. Bee dances provide an excellent example of the _____ of animal communication.

7. Killer whales are unusual in their ability to pass _____ on to their young.

8. Chimpanzees have displayed an ability to invent new _____.

9. Chimpanzees are unable to understand and use _____ in the way that humans do.

10. Humans have a huge advantage over animals because of the human ability to use _____.

TALK *about the* topic

A. Listen to the students talk about animal communication. Read each statement. Then check (☑) who agrees with it. More than one student may agree.

	Hannah	River	Mia	Manny
1. Animals communicate, and they share some communication characteristics with humans.	☐	☐	☐	☐
2. Animal communication is more sophisticated than we understand.	☐	☐	☐	☐
3. Signaling to other animals isn't using displacement.	☐	☐	☐	☐
4. A meerkat looks like a raccoon.	☐	☐	☐	☐

Hannah

River

Mia

Manny

B. Listen to the discussion again. Listen closely for the comments below. Check (☑) the discussion strategy the student uses.

	Expressing an opinion	Agreeing	Asking for clarification or confirmation
1. **River:** "Is that what everyone else got from this lecture?"	☐	☐	☐
2. **Mia:** "Pretty much."	☐	☐	☐
3. **Manny:** "Personally, I think animal communication is a lot more sophisticated than we understand."	☐	☐	☐
4. **Mia:** "How so?"	☐	☐	☐

C. In small groups, discuss one or more of these topics. Try to use the discussion strategies you have learned.

- Manny thinks that animal communication is more sophisticated than most people understand. Do you agree?
- Think of pets you've had or other animals you've interacted with. Could you detect signs of arbitrariness, displacement, cultural transmission, or discreteness in their communication? Give examples.
- The students give several examples of the complexity of human communication. Can you think of others?

REVIEW *your* notes

Use your notes and the following groups of words to make sentences about the lecture. Write them down. Then with a partner, discuss the main ideas of the lecture using your sentences.

sounds, communicate, verbal behavior, nonverbal behavior

arbitrariness, logical relationship, meaning

humans, flexible, wide range, sounds

displacement, physically present, bees

displacement, humans, books, Internet

cultural transmission, generation, killer whales

discreteness, chimpanzees, combine, phrases

discreteness, humans, combine, words, grammar

Now you are ready to take the Unit Test.

TAKE THE UNIT TEST

EXTEND *the* topic

Who can doubt that animals feel and think? If you're still unconvinced they do, the following listening, reading, and research project may change your mind.

A. Listen as researcher Mark Beck fields a student magazine writer's questions about animal emotions.

In small groups, discuss these questions. Share your views with the class.

1. What animals do you think may experience emotions that are similar to human emotions?

2. What feelings do you think animals can communicate? How do they express those feelings?

3. Do you think that animals experience "pure" emotions? Why or why not?

B. An *animal whisperer* is somebody who "communicates" with animals in order to solve their problems. Look at the classified ad of an animal whisperer below and the comments of Dwain Walden that follow.

Katie Black: The Pet Whisperer

"I'll help you connect with your pet!"

- Katie's been "whispering" to pets for 30+ years.
- Not only does she talk to the pets, she also listens! Since the age of three when she got her first pet—a pygmy goat—Katie's been honing her telepathic powers.
- From dogs to lions to rats to donkeys, Katie's counseled them all!
- While Katie prefers to meet the pet in person, she's happy to consult by phone, e-mail, letter, fax, or webcam. She welcomes the most challenging physical, behavioral, and emotional issues.

Yo, dog, what seems to be your problem?
by Dwain Walden

Ever since that movie *The Horse Whisperer* came out, there has been sort of an influx of "whisperers" in the animal kingdom, and I see great potential here for another vocation when I retire from journalism. There are "cat whisperers" and "dog whisperers," etc. They talk secretly to the animals, find out what's on their minds, and may even get their thoughts on global warming.

And, yes, I know that it sounds ridiculous, but there are people with more money than sense, and they will hire these "whisperers" to talk to their animals and then offer them therapy and counsel (the pets and the people). Then the whisperers laugh all the way to the bank.

The bottom line is, you whisper to the dog, and then you poke the dog's nose in your ear and allow your body language to indicate communication is taking place. Then you make up something and tell the owner. In the process, you get your ear cleaned out. That's what they call a win-win situation.

Now discuss these questions in groups of three or four.

1. If you had a pet that needed help, would this ad appeal to you? Why or why not?

2. Based on her ad, what kind of person do you think Katie Black is?

3. Why does Dwain Walden object to animal whisperers? Do you agree with him?

4. Have you or anyone you know had any experience with animal whisperers? Relate it to your group.

C. Choose an animal you are interested in.

- dolphins
- whales
- fish
- birds

- chimpanzees
- monkeys
- gorillas
- polar bears

- meerkats
- cats
- dogs
- your choice

⟶ Use the Internet to investigate your animal's communication behavior.

⟶ Research the following elements:

- How does the animal communicate? Using sounds? Scent? Body language?

- What other animals does it communicate with? Its own species? Other species?

- What meanings does it seem to communicate?

- Analyze its communicative behavior using the four points discussed in this unit's lecture.

⟶ Give a three-minute class presentation based on your research.

UNIT 10

The Evolution of Money

CONNECT *to the* topic

Money—every human society uses it. And every modern society needs it in order to grow and flourish. Through the ages, money has had an ability to change in ways that reflect the culture and technology of the time. Shells, cattle, gold, coins, banknotes, credit cards, e-money—these are just a few of the many forms that money has taken. And now for the first time in human history, most of the money that flows throughout the world is not physical; it is digital information that moves over high-speed cables. While the future forms that money will take are hard to predict, one thing is for sure: Money is here to stay.

What is your attitude toward money? Check (☑) whether you agree or disagree with the following statements.

	Agree	Disagree
It is important to save money every month.	____	____
I prefer to use cash rather than a credit card.	____	____
Having a lot of money is a good thing.	____	____
Money is necessary if we want to help other people.	____	____
I need money to make my dreams come true.	____	____
Money is necessary for a society to grow and develop.	____	____

Think of reasons or examples to support your opinion. Compare responses with a partner.

BUILD *your* vocabulary

A. **The boldfaced words are from this unit's lecture on money. Read along as you listen to each sentence. Then circle the meaning of the boldfaced word.**

1. Large cities began to form in Europe as people **abandoned** farmwork and began other kinds of work. They voluntarily moved to urban areas.

    a. unable to do something

    b. stopped doing something

    c. forced to stop doing something

2. Money was originally a concrete object, like gold, but has become increasingly **abstract**. Now some forms of money are a digital computer code.

    a. separate from physical realities

    b. higher quality

    c. valuable

3. Many of the impressive developments we see in modern **civilization** are due to the creation of money. One example is multinational corporations.

    a. a large city with many businesses

    b. a country with a large population

    c. a society in an advanced state of development

4. There are currently many types of **currency** in the world; yen, pesos, dollars, and euros are just a few.

    a. stocks

    b. precious metals

    c. money

5. When money was invented, it provided **enormous** advantages over previous ways of conducting trade. The differences were huge.

    a. very gradual

    b. completely unexpected

    c. extraordinarily large

6. The wealth of rich children is usually tied to **heredity**. Their money often comes from their parents.

    a. when a parent encourages a child to work hard

    b. when a parent passes on physical possessions to a child

    c. when a parent purchases many expensive things for a child

7. When people believe that hard work will be rewarded, individual **initiative** increases dramatically.

   a. readiness to take action

   b. feelings of tiredness

   c. the desire to become wealthy

8. The value of money is not **subjective**; the value of one dollar in New York is the same as the value of one dollar in California.

   a. changing rapidly and suddenly

   b. not objective

   c. increasing slowly

9. Financial **transactions** involving trillions of dollars take place daily. In the stock market, for example, people exchange shares in hundreds of countries.

   a. interactions between sellers and buyers

   b. profits and losses

   c. putting money into a bank

10. Money has **undergone** tremendous change over the past several thousand years. It now looks very different from the way it once did.

    a. caused or created

    b. experienced or gone through

    c. influenced negatively

B. *INTERACT WITH VOCABULARY!* **Work with a partner. Take turns saying the sentences. Notice the boldfaced words. Reorder the words to make complete sentences. Review any words you don't understand.**

1. (**role** / positive / **played** / money / has / **a** / **in**) billions of people's lives.

2. Money is both physical and digital (of / **at** / **this** / its / **stage** / evolution).

3. (currency / **in** / **fluctuations** / values) affect everyone.

4. Paper money (objects / valuable / **symbolic** / **of** / is) such as gold.

5. Money (a / **of** / as / business / **facilitator** / has acted).

6. Attaining wealth was once (almost / **to** / exclusively / heredity / **tied**).

7. Money allowed entire civilizations (**from** / **away** / to / **move**) agriculture.

8. Modern forms of money allow people (with / to / another / business / one / **out** / **carry**) no matter where they live.

9. Money has been key (the / societies / **of** / modern / **development** / to).

FOCUS _your_ attention

MARKING YOUR NOTES

Taking good notes is one of the first steps to understanding a lecture or presentation. However, it is also important to think about the ideas in the notes. One way of thinking about your notes is to mark them during or after the lecture. Below are some commonly used techniques:

- Underline important ideas.
- Draw stars in the margins to emphasize the most important 5–10 points in the lecture.
- Circle key words and phrases as well as technical vocabulary.
- Draw lines between ideas that have important relationships.
- Write comments to yourself in the margins.
- Write questions about information that you don't clearly understand in the margins.
- Write a short summary statement of the lecture.

The following is an example of how one student marked her notes from a lecture on the influence of money.

What caused them to want independence?

Money led to increases in commerce.

★ Businesses gradually developed → ↑ number of people w. $

★ People wanted independence, so . . .
  - they led the movement toward (democratic values) and gov't.
  - they demanded education for their children

★ democratic govts. + more education = more business and commerce
  = a positive (cycle) had begun—we're still in that cycle

Summary: There's a cycle: $ causes commerce to ↑
↑ commerce = ↑ people having $ and this causes society to Δ
e.g., ↑ freedom and ↑ education . . . = ↑ $ being earned

TRY IT OUT!

A. Listen to this excerpt of a speaker discussing the possibility of a future world currency. Take notes. Then mark your notes using the techniques listed above.

B. Compare notes with a partner. Can you improve them?

LISTEN *to the* lecture

BEFORE YOU LISTEN

You are about to hear this unit's lecture on the evolution of money and the impact of money on society. What are three ways you can pay for goods and services and three ways money influences society?

	Ways to pay	Influences of money
1.		
2.		
3.		

LISTEN FOR MAIN IDEAS

A. Close your book. Listen to the lecture and take notes.

B. Use your notes. Decide if the statements below are *T* (true) or *F* (false), according to the lecture. Correct any false statements.

_____ 1. Barter is a system of direct exchange.

_____ 2. In early societies, landowners possessed most of the wealth.

_____ 3. Money permits people to carry out finanical transactions of any size.

_____ 4. Financial transactions involving money can't be completed quickly.

_____ 5. Money does not move easily across cultural and geographic boundaries.

_____ 6. The value of money is rarely precise.

_____ 7. Money has evolved from being a physical object to an abstract idea.

_____ 8. The rise in commerce was caused by individual initiative.

_____ 9. Money has value independent of the trust and faith that humans place in it.

LISTEN FOR DETAILS

A. Close your book. Listen to the lecture again. Add details to your notes and correct any mistakes.

B. Use your notes. Complete the sentences, based on the lecture.

agriculture	electronic transactions	paper money	social development
brains	manufactured	physical object	working hard
education	more fulfilling	precise	

1. Money can be transferred over any distance in moments using
   electronic transactions

2. Money can be used in exact amounts; thus, one major advantage of money is
   that it is _precise_ .

3. Originally, money was a(n) _physical object_ found in nature, such
   as a cow.

4. Barter was replaced by _manufactured_ physical objects such as
   gold coins.

5. Money first became abstract when gold and silver were replaced
   by _paper money_ .

6. As _____ became more efficient, many people abandoned
   farmwork and moved to cities.

7. When wealth was no longer tied to heredity, having _____
   and _____ became important.

8. The rise of commerce made _____ accessible to more people;
   this helped new businesses grow.

9. Money is a tool that is related to human and _____ .

10. The creation of money has allowed millions of people to live
    _____ lives.

TALK *about the* topic

A. Listen to the students talk about the dangers of credit cards. Read each question. Then check (☑) who answers it.

	Ayman	Molly	Rob	Alana
1. "What happened? Did you lose your card or something?"	☐	☐	☐	☐
2. "How did you find this out?"	☐	☐	☐	☐
3. "So did you have to pay for anything?"	☐	☐	☐	☐

B. Listen to the discussion again. Listen closely for the comments below. Check (☑) the discussion strategy the student uses.

	Expressing an opinion	Agreeing	Offering a fact or example
1. **Ayman:** "It's kind of cool to think that we're seeing money's latest evolution."	☐	☐	☐
2. **Molly:** "My credit card number got stolen sometime last weekend."	☐	☐	☐
3. **Molly:** "The whole episode's just kind of bummed me out."	☐	☐	☐
4. **Alana:** "I don't blame you . . . "	☐	☐	☐

> **Discussion Strategy: Agreeing** Observe a group discussion, and you're likely to hear expressions of agreement like *Uh-huh, Right, Yes!, I agree, Exactly!,* and *No doubt.* Agreeing is great way to support another speaker, either in casual conversation or to build an alliance when an issue is being discussed.

C. In small groups, discuss one or more of these topics. Try to use the discussion strategies you have learned.

- Do you think that cash is safer than using credit cards or electronic money?
- Do you think that it is safe to shop on the Internet?
- Would you react similarly to Molly if your credit card number were stolen?

REVIEW *your* notes

Read your notes. Work with a partner and take turns explaining the ideas from the lecture. Give examples or add comments as you discuss. Then complete the notes below.

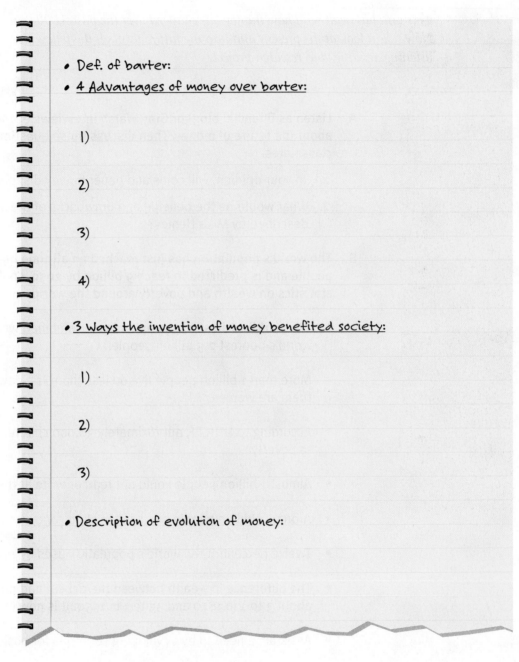

- Def. of barter:
- <u>4 Advantages of money over barter:</u>

    1)

    2)

    3)

    4)

- <u>3 Ways the invention of money benefited society:</u>

    1)

    2)

    3)

- Description of evolution of money:

TAKE THE UNIT TEST

Now you are ready to take the Unit Test.

EXTEND *the* topic

This unit has dealt with how money has changed over the past 5,000 years. Now take a look at the present and into the future through the following listening, reading, and research project.

A. **Listen as financial blogger Gray Walsh interviews economist Mika Henley about the future of money. Then discuss these questions with your classmates.**

1. In your opinion, will coins and paper money disappear in the near future?

2. What would be the benefits and drawbacks of the future world of money described by Mika Henley?

B. **The world's population has just reached an all-time high of 6.6 billion people and is predicted to reach 9 billion by 2050. Look at the following statistics on wealth and poverty around the world.**

- The world's richest 225 people have a combined wealth equal to the world's poorest 2.5 billion people.

- More than 1 billion people live on less than $1 a day, and 70 percent of them are women.

- According to UNICEF, approximately 30,000 children die each day due to poverty.

- Almost 1 billion people could not read or write at the turn of this century.

- Around 1 billion people are living in slum conditions.

- Twelve percent of the world's population uses 85 percent of its water.

- The difference in wealth between the richest and poorest countries was about 3 to 1 in 1820 and 35 to 1 in 1950. It is now over 70 to 1.

- Assistance needed by developing countries for basic education: $6 billion

- Assistance needed by developing countries for water and sanitation: $9 billion

- Assistance needed by developing countries for reproductive health for women: $12 billion

- Assistance needed by developing countries for basic health and nutrition: $13 billion

- Current spending on cosmetics in the United States.: $8 billion

- Current spending on ice cream in Europe: $11 billion

- Current spending on business entertainment in Japan: $35 billion

- Current spending on military in the world: $780 billion

Discuss these questions with a partner.

1. Why do you think the gap between the wealthy and the poor continues to widen?

2. How can governments address the widening gap?

C. Choose one of the following topics and a specific time period.

- families
- education
- transportation
- communication

- health care
- science
- entertainment

---> Prepare a presentation on what has changed.

---> Speculate on how it will look in the future.

UNIT 11

The Fountain of Youth

CONNECT *to the* topic

Living forever. The possibility has intrigued philosophers, scientists, and novelists for thousands of years. Although living forever is not possible, ways to extend the human lifespan to 100 years and beyond are the object of a great deal of scientific research. To date, the results indicate that it may one day be possible for many people to live well past the age of 100. However, as people live longer, they will have to find a balance between the length and the quality of their lives.

Although modern cultures tend to glorify youth, there are both advantages and disadvantages to aging. In groups, list some of those advantages and disadvantages.

Advantages	Disadvantages
---> _____	---> _____
---> _____	---> _____
---> _____	---> _____

As a class, discuss your results.

BUILD *your* vocabulary

A. **The boldfaced words are from this unit's lecture on aging. Read along as you listen to each sentence. Then circle the meaning of the boldfaced word.**

1. Some lifestyles **accelerate** the aging process by damaging the body.

    a. increase the speed of something

    b. cause something to develop slowly

    c. make something easier to notice

2. If our body doesn't get rid of waste products, they will **accumulate** inside our cells. In turn, we can become tired or even sick, and can't function as well.

    a. move from one place to another

    b. remove

    c. gradually increase in quantity or size

3. Scientists—particularly **biologists**—are intrigued by the aging process.

    a. people who study living things

    b. people who study the natural forces of light and heat

    c. people who study the composition of synthetic substances

4. Because a half-cup serving of ice cream typically has 120-plus **calories**, eating too much of it can cause weight gain.

    a. large amounts of processed sugar

    b. units measuring the amount of energy in food

    c. parts of some foods that increase muscle mass

5. Our body is made up of millions of **cells**, with new ones produced daily.

    a. tiny organisms that are important to health

    b. parts of a person's DNA

    c. the smallest parts of a living thing that can exist independently

6. Mice whose bodies produce extra **electrons** age faster.

    a. heat

    b. electricity

    c. matter in an atom

7. People with a fast **metabolism** tend to be thin, even if they eat a great deal.

    a. an intense type of aerobic exercise

    b. the chemical process that changes food into energy

    c. the rate at which a person breathes

8. Salt **molecules** are made up of two parts: sodium and chloride.

   a. fluids that have become solid

   b. the smallest units of matter that have a unique chemical nature

   c. the parts of food that give it flavor

9. One benefit of getting proper **nutrition**—including eating protein and a variety of fruits and vegetables—is living a longer life.

   a. the balance of food a person consumes

   b. food that has not been processed in a factory

   c. a diet that does not include any red meat

10. One way to **supplement** our diet is to take vitamins.

   a. add something to improve a situation

   b. use one thing in place of another

   c. simplify something

B. *INTERACT WITH VOCABULARY!* **Work with a partner. Take turns completing each sentence with the correct form of the word. Notice the boldfaced words. Read the completed sentences aloud. Review any words you don't understand.**

accumulated	accumulating	accumulation

1. _____ evidence indicates that we **have the potential to** control our rate of aging.

2. The _____ of waste products in our cells has a **negative impact** on our bodies.

accelerated	accelerating	acceleration

3. Smoking causes cell damage, and cell damage is **consistent with** _____ aging.

4. One **interpretation of** scientific research is that the _____ of our aging process is part of our body's design.

nutrition	nutrients	nutritious

5. Our lifespan is **affected by** the _____ that are in our food.

6. A diet that restricts **caloric intake** can still be _____.

FOCUS *your* attention

PROBLEM–SOLUTION RELATIONSHIPS

In some academic lectures, the speaker's goal is to describe problems and possible solutions to those problems. In this type of lecture, it is important to first clearly distinguish the problems, then determine which solutions apply to which problems.

Expressing problems:

> *The first problem is . . .*
> *The bad news is . . .*
> *This causes problems such as . . .*
> *One theory of (the problem) says . . .*
> *Think about the implication . . .*

Expressing reasons for problems:

> *The first reason is . . .*
> *A second major reason is . . .*
> *This is caused by . . .*
> *This, in turn, causes . . .*
> *This happens because . . .*
> *One interpretation is . . .*

Expressing solutions:

> *What can be done about this?*
> *How can we solve this problem?*
> *There is some good news here . . .*
> *Is there any good news here?*
> *One possible solution is . . .*

TRY IT OUT!

A. Listen to this excerpt of a health instructor addressing causes of aging skin and solutions. Take notes. Try to organize your notes so that the problems and their solutions are clearly related.

B. Compare notes with a partner. Can you improve your notes?

LISTEN *to the* lecture

BEFORE YOU LISTEN

You are about to hear this unit's lecture on aging. What do you think are the top two causes of aging? What are two ways we might slow the aging process?

1. _____

2. _____

3. _____

4. _____

LISTEN FOR MAIN IDEAS

A. **Close your book. Listen to the lecture and take notes.**

B. **Use your notes. Complete these main ideas, based on the lecture.**

calorie restriction	fifty	imbalance	oxygen
damage theories	high-tech	natural	program theories

1. _____ are based on the idea that our bodies are designed to live for a limited amount of time.

2. _____ concern the idea that aging occurs because of cellular damage.

3. The Hayflick Limit theory is based on research indicating that some cells only divide about _____ times.

4. The only known way to consistently increase life-span is _____.

5. Free radicals cause aging by creating a(n) _____.

6. The key to reducing free radicals is to metabolize less _____.

7. Two approaches to slowing aging are the _____ approach and the _____ approach.

LISTEN FOR DETAILS

A. **Close your book. Listen to the lecture again. Add details to your notes and correct any mistakes.**

B. **Use your notes. Circle the letter of the phrase that best completes each idea, according to the lecture.**

1. Why were early damage theories incorrect?

   a. because damage is not an important cause of aging

   b. because damage occurs only temporarily

   c. because the human body has the capacity to repair itself

2. What is one interpretation of the Hayflick Limit theory?

   a. Our DNA gradually becomes damaged.

   b. A cellular clock exists in our DNA.

   c. DNA can potentially divide for fifty years.

3. What directly affects the rate of cell division?

   a. the amount of waste products in the cell

   b. the amount of exercise a person gets

   c. the amount of food a person eats

4. By how much should a person reduce his calorie intake if he adopts a CR diet?

   a. 20 percent

   b. 30 percent

   c. 40 percent

5. What is one environmental factor that causes free radicals to form?

   a. strong sunlight

   b. oxygen

   c. air pollution

6. Which of the following is *not* damaged by free radicals?

   a. DNA

   b. cell membranes

   c. electrons

7. What is xenotransplantation?

   a. using drugs that reduce the metabolic rate

   b. using animal tissues to treat human illnesses

   c. using stem cells to repair human organs

TALK *about the* topic

A. Listen to the students talk about ways to slow aging. Read each opinion. Then check (☑) who disagrees with it. Move than one student may disagree.

	Hannah	Manny	River	Mia
1. Everybody knows that the natural approach will slow down the aging process.	☐	☐	☐	☐
2. People don't know what they can do to slow aging.	☐	☐	☐	☐
3. I'd be willing to cut back my diet by 30 percent.	☐	☐	☐	☐

B. Listen to the discussion again. Listen closely for the comments below. Check (☑) the discussion strategy the student uses.

	Asking for opinions or ideas	Disagreeing	Asking for clarification or confirmation
1. **Mia:** "Huh?"	☐	☐	☐
2. **Hannah:** "I'm not so sure about that."	☐	☐	☐
3. **Hannah:** "So what then?"	☐	☐	☐
4. **Mia:** "Can I clarify something from earlier in the lecture?"	☐	☐	☐

> **Discussion Strategy: Asking for clarification or confirmation** To clarify means to make clearer. To confirm is to remove doubt. You can clarify or confirm by restating what you understood: *You mean . . .* or *Do you mean . . . ?* Or you can ask open-ended questions like *What do you mean?* and *Could you clarify . . . ?*

C. In small groups, discuss one or more of these topics. Try to use the discussion strategies you have learned.

- Do you agree with River that the natural approach is the best way to live longer?
- Do you believe that your life span is predetermined?
- Do you agree with Manny's feeling that most people know how to live a healthy life, but don't act on it?

REVIEW *your* notes

Use your notes. Work with a partner. Complete the chart as you discuss the theories and main ideas covered in the lecture.

Theory category	Specific theory	Key terms	Causes of aging—solutions
program theories		cellular waste products metabolic rate	
damage theories		free radicals	

Now you are ready to take the Unit Test.

TAKE THE UNIT TEST

Tip!

Notes that are organized in categories—in a chart, for example—are easier to review. Clean, organized notes can make information more approachable.

EXTEND *the* topic

Of the ideas on aging that you've heard, has one in particular appealed to you? Maybe you'll connect to one of the ideas in the following listening, reading, and research project.

A. Listen as student health reporter Sara Sandlin interviews Professor Dominica Pirelli, an anti-aging researcher, about the effects of a positive mental outlook on aging. Then discuss these questions with your classmates.

1. Do you agree that a positive attitude is related to general health? Why?

2. Do you agree that a positive attitude can increase your life span? Why?

B. Some people, known as centenarians, live to be 100 years old and beyond. Read these short profiles about three centenarians and their tips for living a long life.

Jeanne Calment, 122 years old

At the age of twenty-one, Jeanne married a wealthy store owner, so she never had to work. She maintained an active lifestyle nearly her entire life by playing tennis, cycling, and playing the piano. At the age of eighty-five she began fencing, and she rode a bicycle until she was 110. She attributed her long life to regularly eating olive oil, which she put on nearly all of her food and rubbed on her skin.

Yone Minagawa, 114 years old

Yone Minagawa lived a busy life in which she sold flowers and vegetables at a coal mine and raised five children after her husband died. She enjoyed playing the shamisen, a Japanese musical instrument. And even when she was 114, she participated in club activities in a wheelchair and "danced" along to music. She liked sweets and was particularly fond of Japanese cakes filled with sweet bean paste. Ms. Minagawa said that her long life was due to a good diet and getting a good night's sleep.

Antonio Todde, 112 years old

Antonio Todde was the third of twelve children in a poor shepherd family. His parents and two sisters lived into their nineties. Mr. Todde attended school for only one year. For sixty-five years of his life, he walked a great deal as he followed flocks of sheep up and down the steep mountain paths near his home. Mr. Todde attributed his longevity to drinking a glass of Sardinian red wine every day. He once said, "Just love your brother and drink a glass of good wine." In addition to the wine, he regularly ate pork, lamb, pasta, and soup.

Discuss the following questions with your classmates.

1. What do you think about the lifestyles of these three centenarians?

2. What would be the advantages and disadvantages of living to 100 or beyond?

C. Use the Internet or library to research a natural or high-tech approach to extending human life.

⫯ Choose a topic:

Natural approaches	High-tech approaches
raw food	tissue engineering
exercise	stem cells
vitamins	xenotransplantations
blueberries	human growth hormone
laughter	light therapy

⫯ Include the following elements in your presentation:

- the ease of using this approach

- the expense of this approach

- examples or evidence of the effectiveness of this approach

- why you would or would not use this approach

⫯ Give a class presentation based on your research.

UNIT 12

Marriage

CONNECT *to the* topic

Why do people get married? While many people today might answer "for love," the answer to this question is complex. People marry for many different reasons, and many forms of marriage exist in the world. Also, ideas about marriage can change radically in any society over the course of even a single generation. This can be seen in the many ways some parents and children disagree about issues such as who and when to marry, and what type of wedding ceremony to have. Despite all of the complexities, however, one thing seems certain: People will still be getting married for many years to come.

Look at the following characteristics. Which do you think are most important in a marriage partner? Rank the items from 1 to 5, with 1 being the most important characteristic. Survey two classmates. Add the numbers and divide by three to get the average.

Characteristic:	Good looks	Kindness	Wealth	Nationality	Intelligence
My rankings:	☐	☐	☐	☐	☐
Classmate A's rankings:	☐	☐	☐	☐	☐
Classmate B's rankings:	☐	☐	☐	☐	☐

Compare results with the rest of your class.

BUILD *your* vocabulary

A. The boldfaced words are from this unit's lecture on marriage. Listen to each sentence. Then guess the meaning of the boldfaced words. Work with a partner.

1. Most people don't get married until they've reached **adulthood**. Marriages involving children and young teenagers are rare in most parts of the world.

2. Naomi heard that many women are delaying marriage until after they turn thirty. She **confirmed** that information by checking the Internet.

3. As people from many countries meet and develop relationships, the number of **interracial** marriages increases.

4. Married couples enjoy a kind of **legitimacy**, while unmarried couples may be considered outside the accepted standards of society.

5. Saed has **matured** a lot since moving out of his parents' house. He's become very responsible and is able to take care of himself.

6. **Nationalistic barriers** to international marriages are gradually disappearing because meeting someone from a different country is fairly common.

7. One societal **norm** of marriage is that people are expected to marry someone of a similar age. Many people view large differences in age as strange.

8. Growth in the Hispanic **population** in parts of the United States has caused the number of marriages between Hispanics and whites to rise.

9. One strong reason for marriage in many cultures is a woman becoming **pregnant**. It is important that the child has a father and mother to care for it.

10. My parents are from the same **social class**. They lived in similar neighborhoods, and their parents' incomes were nearly the same.

B. Match each word to the correct definition.

a.	adulthood	d.	legitimacy	g.	norm	i.	pregnant
b.	confirmed	e.	matured	h.	population	j.	social class
c.	interracial	f.	nationalistic barriers				

1. ___ when a woman is carrying an unborn offspring in her body

2. ___ fully developed and behaving in a reasonable way; not childish

3. ___ a block people face because of their national beliefs

4. ___ between different races of people

5. ___ people in a particular area or members of a particular group

6. ___ determined that something is definitely true

7. ___ the period of life when a person is completely grown

8. ___ acceptance, validity

9. ___ a group of people with a similar rank in society

10. ___ the usual or acceptable way of doing something

C. Say each word to yourself. Write *N* if it is a noun, *V* if it is a verb, and *A* if it is an adjective.

1. ___ adulthood
2. ___ confirmed
3. ___ interracial
4. ___ legitimacy
5. ___ matured

6. ___ nationalistic barriers
7. ___ norm
8. ___ population
9. ___ pregnant
10. ___ social class

D. *INTERACT WITH VOCABULARY!* Work with a partner. Take turns completing each sentence with the correct form of the word. Notice the boldfaced words. Read the completed sentences aloud. Review any words you don't understand.

confirm	confirmed	confirmation

1. Researchers have _____ that caring for children properly is important to the **survival of** any society.

2. Research showing that married couples are healthier than single people is _____ of the **benefits of** marriage.

legitimate	legitimately	legitimacy

3. Children need to be _____ **linked to** their father.

4. One of the **functions of** marriage is to give the couple _____ in the eyes of society.

mature	maturity	maturation

5. As couples _____, they become **similar to** one another.

6. Greater _____ can result in a **rise in** tolerance toward people of other races.

nations	national	nationalistic

7. The tax policies of _____ governments can provide **pressure for** young people to get married.

8. In most _____, marriages are legally **recognized by** the government.

FOCUS *your* attention

PERSONAL REACTIONS TO TOPICS

Taking good notes is a crucial part of understanding a lecture, but it is also important to actively think about the notes. Here are ways you can do this:

- Add examples from your own life.
- Agree and disagree with information in the lecture.
- Suggest an alternative point of view.
- Consider the implications of information in the lecture.
- Provide additional reasons for something.
- Consider the strengths and weaknesses of a position or situation.
- Predict how the situation will change in the future.

Considering the information in the lecture from various points of view and making a personal connection with that information will help you 1) understand and remember the information better, 2) clarify what you do not understand, and 3) create a more unified understanding of the topic. In short, reacting to the information in your notes is as important as taking high-quality notes.

TRY IT OUT!

A. **Listen to this excerpt of a speech discussing marriage in Europe. Complete the notes below.**

B. **Compare notes and reactions with a partner.**

C. **React to the information in your notes by using some of the approaches described above.**

Love and marriage

- A new idea _____

- Up to 300 years ago _____

- People lived and worked _____

Marriage = _____

Economic reason = external motivation for marriage

Internal motivation for marriage = _____

LISTEN *to the* lecture

BEFORE YOU LISTEN

You are about to listen to this unit's lecture on marriage. Think of two benefits of marriage and two criteria that people use for choosing a marriage partner.

Two benefits of marriage: _____

_____

Two criteria for choosing a partner: _____

_____

LISTEN FOR MAIN IDEAS

A. **Close your book. Listen to the lecture and take notes.**

B. **Use your notes. Select the best answer, based on the lecture.**

1. Some form of marriage exists in _____.

   a. a few societies

   b. most societies

   c. every society

2. A universal benefit of marriage is that it creates _____.

   a. individual wealth

   b. relationships between families

   c. social harmony

3. Marriage increases the likelihood that _____.

   a. children will be cared for

   b. families will be economically successful

   c. society will develop rapidly

4. In most societies marriage establishes _____.

   a. the parents' legal status

   b. the children's caretakers

   c. the rights of children

5. Homogamy means that people marry _____.

   a. someone similar to themselves

   b. someone chosen by their parents

   c. someone only after a long courtship

6. The strongest major trend in marriages of the future is a decline

   in _____.

   a. religious homogamy

   b. racial homogamy

   c. educational homogamy

7. Interracial marriages in the United States are increasing because of increases

   in the _____ populations.

   a. African-American and white

   b. Asian and white

   c. Asian and Hispanic

LISTEN FOR DETAILS

A. Close your book. Listen to the lecture again. Add details to your notes and correct any mistakes.

B. Use your notes. Decide if the statements below are *T* (true) or *F* (false), according to the lecture. Correct any false statements.

____ 1. Anthropologists agree that marriage is the union of two or more people who are legally recognized by the government.

____ 2. The alliance theory states that marriage increases social cooperation.

____ 3. Because of the slow development of human children, they need the protection of their parents for a relatively long time.

____ 4. The legitimacy argument states that a child must be legally linked to his or her mother.

____ 5. According to the lecturer, 75 percent of Americans marry someone from the same racial group.

____ 6. Since 1980, the number of interracial marriages in the United States has remained steady.

____ 7. A recent poll indicated that African Americans showed the greatest acceptance of their grandchildren marrying someone of a different race.

TALK *about the* topic

A. Listen to the students talk about modern marriage. Read each anecdote. Then check (☑) who identifies with it.

	Michael	Yhinny	Qiang	May
1. My family is conservative.	☐	☐	☐	☐
2. I'm used to seeing mixed marriages.	☐	☐	☐	☐
3. I know a lot of couples who are living together unmarried.	☐	☐	☐	☐

B. Listen to the discussion again. Listen closely for the comments below. Check (☑) the discussion strategy the student uses.

	Expressing an opinion	Offering a fact or example	Paraphrasing
1. **Michael:** "So in other words, in your parents' generation you see a lot of homogamy, but not in ours?"	☐	☐	☐
2. **Qiang:** "You know what I find fascinating . . . "	☐	☐	☐
3. **Michael:** "Even here, generally, couples are expected to get married."	☐	☐	☐
4. **Yhinny:** "I think big changes are ahead!"	☐	☐	☐

> **Discussion Strategy: Offering a fact or example** By offering a fact or example, you can transform a topic from theory to reality. This can make the topic not only more understandable, but also more memorable. You can use examples from personal experiences (*In my experience . . .*), observations (*I've noticed . . .*), and media (*I just read this article in* The Times *. . .*).

C. In small groups discuss one or more of these topics. Try to use the discussion strategies you have learned.

- Do you agree with Yhinny that many young couples today are not homogenous?
- Qiang says that "in many cultures, marriage seems to be less and less important every day." How would most people in your country react to this statement?
- How do you think marriage will change in the next fifty years?

REVIEW *your* notes

Work in pairs. React to these ideas from the lecture. Use your notes and the ideas listed in Focus Your Attention to add comments below. What do you agree or disagree with? Can you add different ideas or reasons? What are the implications of the information in the lecture?

Effects of marriage on social cooperation:

Effects of marriage on child care:

Establishment of children's legal rights:

Marriage partner and social class:

Marriage partner and racial group:

Marriage partner and educational level:

Future of marriage and racial homogamy:

Now you are ready to take the Unit Test.

Tip!

Reacting to lecture information and adding those thoughts to your notes is a great practice. You will not only better remember the material, but also develop a personal connection to it.

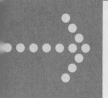

EXTEND *the* topic

As the lecturer's tone indicated, the concept of marriage is widely supported. Learn more about why that is in the following listening and reading exercises. Then do your own research on the topic.

A. Listen as HealthTV guest and anthropologist Dr. Sharon Wright discusses the effects of marriage on health. Then discuss these questions in small groups.

1. Can you think of reasons not mentioned by Dr. Wright why marriage is beneficial for some people's health?

2. In what situations might marriage be harmful to a person's health?

B. Read these three perspectives on the future of marriage.

Harlan Fidell, sociologist: Although I'll admit that marriage has served a purpose throughout much of human history, the era of marriage is nearly finished. Divorce rates skyrocketed in the 1960s and they're still high today. Marriage will be a thing of the past within the next fifty years. Actually, the only thing that keeps marriage alive is the legal system. Once laws are changed so that they don't favor married people, we'll see a rapid decline in the number of marriages.

Sasha Becker, journalist: The future of marriage is here. Both now and in the immediate future we'll see a mix of married and single people. In countries where the economy is strong, we'll see rises in the number of single people. For instance, by 2020, 30 percent of the households in the United States will be what we call solo singles. However, none of this means that marriage will disappear. The majority of people will be married at some point in their lives.

Ted Marcus, marriage counselor: Marriage? I can't imagine a society without it. Marriage will enjoy a resurgence in many Western countries as we continue to learn more about how to make marriage work well and educate young people about marriage. We now know a lot about how to make good, long-lasting relationships, but we've done a poor job of communicating that information to high school and university students. Once we get better at the education side of things, we'll see more and more successful marriages and that will increase the attractiveness of marriage to young single people.

In groups, consider these questions. Then discuss the reasons for your answers.

1. Which view do you most agree with?

2. Which trend best describes the future of marriage in your home country?

C. A recent poll of approximately 2,000 Americans revealed the top ten personal qualities that people consider necessary for a successful marriage.

⟶ Consider the qualities listed below.

commitment	compassion	honesty	love	support
communication	dependability	humor	respect	trust

⟶ Decide which of these qualities you would select as your top three.

⟶ Come up with some qualities that you would add to the list.

⟶ Discuss as a class.

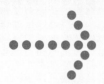

APPENDIX A: academic word list

Numbers indicate the sublist of the Academic Word List. For example, *abandon* and its family members are in Sublist 8. Sublist 1 contains the most frequent words in the list, and Sublist 10 contains the least frequent. **Boldfacing** indicates that the word is taught in *Contemporary Topic 3*. The page number of the section where the word is taught is indicated in parentheses.

abandon (p. 93)	8	anticipate	9	bulk	9	compile	10
abstract (p. 93)	6	apparent	4	capable	6	complement	8
academy	5	append	8	capacity	5	complex	2
access	4	appreciate	8	category	2	component	3
accommodate	9	approach	1	cease	9	compound	5
accompany	8	appropriate	2	challenge	5	comprehensive	7
accumulate (p. 103)	8	approximate	4	channel	7	comprise	7
accurate	6	arbitrary	8	chapter	2	compute	2
achieve	2	area	1	chart	8	conceive	10
acknowledge	6	aspect	2	**chemical** (p. 43)	7	concentrate	4
acquire	2	assemble	10	circumstance	3	concept	1
adapt	7	assess	1	cite	6	conclude	2
adequate	4	assign	6	**civil** (p. 73)	4	concurrent	9
adjacent	10	assist	2	clarify	8	conduct	2
adjust	5	assume	1	classic	7	confer	4
administrate	2	assure	9	clause	5	confine	9
adult (p. 113)	7	**attach** (p. 53)	6	code	4	**confirm** (p. 113)	7
advocate	7	**attain** (p. 23)	9	coherent	9	conflict	5
affect	2	**attitude** (p. 3)	4	coincide	9	conform	8
aggregate	6	attribute	4	collapse	10	consent	3
aid	7	author	6	colleague	10	consequent	2
albeit	10	authority	1	commence	9	considerable	3
allocate	6	automate	8	comment	3	**consist** (p. 13)	1
alter	5	available	1	commission	2	**constant** (p. 3)	3
alternative	3	aware	5	commit	4	constitute	1
ambiguous	8	behalf	9	commodity	8	constrain	3
amend	5	**benefit** (p. 103)	1	communicate	4	**construct** (p. 3)	2
analogy	9	bias	8	community	2	consult	5
analyze	1	bond	6	compatible	9	**consume** (p. 23)	2
annual	4	brief	6	compensate	3	contact	5

contemporary	8	despite	4	ensure	3	fluctuate	8
context	1	**detect** (p. 63)	8	entity	5	focus	2
contract	1	deviate	8	environment	1	format	9
contradict	8	device	9	equate	2	formula	1
contrary	7	**devote** (p. 13)	9	equip	7	forthcoming	10
contrast	4	differentiate	7	equivalent	5	found	9
contribute	3	dimension	4	erode	9	foundation	7
controversy (p. 73)	9	diminish	9	error	4	framework	3
convene	3	**discrete** (p. 83)	5	establish	1	**function** (p. 103)	1
converse	9	discriminate	6	estate	6	fund	3
convert	7	displace	8	estimate	1	fundamental	5
convince	10	display	6	ethic	9	furthermore	6
cooperate	6	dispose	7	ethnic	4	gender	6
coordinate	3	**distinct** (p. 83)	2	evaluate	2	generate	5
core	3	distort	9	eventual	8	**generation** (p. 83)	5
corporate	3	distribute	1	evident	1	**globe** (p. 23)	7
correspond	3	diverse	6	**evolve** (p. 3)	5	goal	4
couple (p. 113)	7	document	3	exceed	6	grade	7
create	1	domain	6	exclude	3	grant	4
credit	2	domestic	4	**exhibit** (p. 13)	8	**guarantee** (p. 33)	7
criteria	3	dominate	3	**expand** (p. 3)	5	guideline	8
crucial	8	draft	5	expert	6	hence	4
culture	2	drama	8	explicit	6	**hierarchy** (p. 23)	7
currency (p. 93)	8	duration	9	exploit	8	highlight	8
cycle	4	dynamic	7	export	1	hypothesis	4
data	1	economy	1	expose	5	identical	7
debate	4	edit	6	external	5	**identify** (p. 3)	1
decade (p. 43)	7	element	2	extract	7	**ideology** (p. 33)	7
decline	5	eliminate	7	**facilitate** (p. 63)	5	ignorance	6
deduce	3	emerge	4	factor	1	illustrate	3
define	1	emphasis	3	feature	2	image	5
definite	7	empirical	7	federal	6	immigrate	3
demonstrate	3	**enable** (p. 33)	5	fee	6	impact	2
denote	8	encounter	10	file	7	implement	4
deny	7	energy	5	final	2	implicate	4
depress	10	enforce	5	finance	1	**implicit** (p. 43)	8
derive	1	**enhance** (p. 53)	6	finite	7	imply	3
design	2	**enormous** (p. 93)	10	**flexible** (p. 63)	6	impose	4

incentive	6	investigate	4	minimal	9	parallel	4
incidence	6	**invoke** (p. 53)	10	minimize	8	parameter	4
incline	10	involve	1	minimum	6	participate	2
income (p. 23)	1	isolate	7	ministry	6	partner	3
incorporate	6	issue	1	minor	3	passive	9
index	6	item	2	mode	7	perceive	2
indicate	1	job	4	modify	5	percent	1
individual	1	journal	2	monitor	5	period	1
induce	8	justify	3	**motive** (p. 13)	6	persist	10
inevitable (p. 3)	8	label	4	**mutual** (p. 53)	9	perspective	5
infer	7	labor	1	negate	3	phase	4
infrastructure	8	layer	3	network	5	**phenomenon** (p. 3)	7
inherent	9	lecture	6	neutral	6	philosophy	3
inhibit	6	legal	1	nevertheless	6	physical	3
initial	3	legislate	1	nonetheless	10	**plus** (p. 103)	8
initiate (p. 93)	6	levy	10	**norm** (p. 113)	9	policy	1
injure	2	liberal	5	normal	2	portion	9
innovate	7	license	5	notion	5	pose	10
input	6	likewise	10	notwithstanding	10	positive	2
insert	7	link	3	nuclear	8	potential	2
insight	9	locate	3	objective	5	practitioner	8
inspect	8	**logic** (p. 43)	5	obtain	2	precede	6
instance	3	**maintain** (p. 63)	2	obvious	4	**precise** (p. 83)	5
institute	2	major	1	occupy	4	predict	4
instruct	6	**manipulate** (p. 43)	8	occur	1	**predominant** (p. 13)	8
integral	9	manual	9	odd	10	preliminary	9
integrate	4	margin	5	offset	8	presume	6
integrity	10	**mature** (p. 113)	9	ongoing	10	previous	2
intelligence	6	maximize	3	option	4	primary	2
intense	8	mechanism	4	orient	5	prime	5
interact	3	**media** (p. 33)	7	outcome	3	principal	4
intermediate	9	mediate	9	output	4	principle	1
internal	4	medical	5	overall	4	prior	4
interpret	1	medium	9	overlap	9	priority	7
interval	6	mental	5	overseas	6	proceed	1
intervene	7	method	1	panel	10	process	1
intrinsic	10	migrate	6	paradigm	7	professional	4
invest	2	military	9	paragraph	8	prohibit	7

project	4	respond	1	stable	5	thesis	7
promote (p. 33)	4	restore	8	statistic	4	topic	7
proportion	3	restrain	9	**status** (p. 23)	4	trace	6
prospect (p. 53)	8	restrict	2	straightforward	10	tradition	2
protocol	9	**retain** (p. 43)	4	**strategy** (p. 13)	2	transfer	2
psychology (p. 43)	5	reveal	6	stress	4	transform	6
publication	7	revenue	5	structure	1	transit	5
publish	3	reverse	7	style	5	transmit	7
purchase	2	revise	8	submit	7	transport	6
pursue	5	revolution	9	subordinate	9	trend	5
qualitative	9	rigid	9	subsequent	4	trigger	9
quote	7	role	1	subsidy	6	**ultimate** (p. 83)	7
radical	8	route	9	substitute	5	**undergo** (p. 93)	10
random (p. 83)	8	scenario	9	successor	7	**underlie** (p. 13)	6
range	2	schedule	8	sufficient	3	undertake	4
ratio	5	scheme	3	sum	4	uniform	8
rational	6	scope	6	summary	4	unify	9
react	3	section	1	**supplement** (p. 103)	9	unique	7
recover	6	sector	1	survey	2	utilize	6
refine	9	**secure** (p. 73)	2	survive	7	valid	3
regime	4	seek	2	suspend	9	vary	1
region	2	select	2	**sustain** (p. 63)	5	**vehicle** (p. 63)	8
register	3	sequence	3	**symbol** (p. 23)	5	version	5
regulate	2	series	4	tape	6	**via** (p. 73)	8
reinforce (p. 3)	8	sex	3	target	5	violate	9
reject	5	shift	3	task	3	virtual	8
relax	9	significant	1	team	9	visible	7
release (p. 43)	7	similar	1	technical	3	vision	9
relevant	2	simulate	7	**technique** (p. 73)	3	visual	8
reluctance	10	site	2	technology	3	volume	3
rely (p. 63)	3	so-called	10	**temporary** (p. 43)	9	voluntary	7
remove	3	sole	7	tense	8	welfare	5
require	1	somewhat	7	terminate	8	whereas	5
research	1	source	1	text	2	whereby	10
reside	2	specific	1	theme	8	**widespread** (p. 3)	8
resolve	4	specify	3	theory	1		
resource (p. 63)	2	sphere	9	thereby	8		

APPENDIX B: affix charts

Learning the meanings of affixes can help you identify unfamiliar words you read or hear. A *prefix* is a letter or group of letters at the beginning of a word. It usually changes the meaning. A *suffix* is a letter or group of letters at the end of a word. It usually changes the part of speech.

The charts below and on page 127 contain common prefixes and suffixes. Refer to the charts as you use this book.

Prefixes

PREFIX	MEANING	EXAMPLE
a-, ab-, il-, im-, in-, ir-, un-	not, without	atypical, abnormal illegal, impossible, inconvenient, irregular, unfair
anti-	opposed to, against	antisocial, antiseptic
co-, col-, com-, con-, cor-	with, together	coexist, collect, commune, connect, correlate
de-	give something the opposite quality	decriminalize
dis-	not, remove	disapprove, disarm
ex-	no longer, former	ex-wife, ex-president
ex-	out, from	export, exit
extra-	outside, beyond	extracurricular, extraordinary
im-, in-	in, into	import, incoming
inter-	between, among	international
post-	later than, after	postgraduate
pro-	in favor of	pro-education
semi-	half, partly	semicircle, semi-literate
sub-	under, below, less important	subway, submarine, subordinate
super-	larger, greater, stronger	supermarket, supervisor

Suffixes

SUFFIX	MEANING	EXAMPLE
-able, -ible	having the quality of, capable of (adj)	comfortable, responsible
-al, -ial	relating to (adj)	professional, ceremonial
-ance, -ence, -ancy, -ency	the act, state, or quality of (n)	performance, intelligence conservancy, competency
-ation, -tion, -ion	the act, state, or result of (n)	examination, selection, facilitation
-ar, -er, -or, -ist	someone who does a particular thing (n)	beggar, photographer, editor, psychologist
-ful	full of (adj)	beautiful, harmful, fearful
-ify, -ize	give something a particular quality (v)	clarify, modernize
-ility	the quality of (n)	affordability, responsibility, humility
-ism	a political or religious belief system (n)	atheism, capitalism
-ist	relating to (or someone who has) a political or religious belief (adj, n)	Buddhist, socialist
-ious, -ive, -ous,	having a particular quality (adj)	mysterious, creative, dangerous
-ity	a particular quality (n)	popularity, creativity
-less	without (adj)	careless, worthless
-ly	in a particular way (adj., adv.)	briefly, fluently
-ment	conditions that result from something (n)	government, development
-ness	quality of (n)	happiness, seriousness

CD: tracking guide

TRACK	ACTIVITY	PAGE
CD 1		
1	Introduction	
UNIT 1		
2	Build Your Vocabulary	3
3	Try It Out!	5
4	Listen for Main Ideas and Listen for Details	6–7
5	Talk About the Topic, Parts A and B	8
6	Take the Unit Test	9
7	Extend the Topic, Part A	10
UNIT 2		
8	Build Your Vocabulary	13
9	Try It Out!	15
10	Listen for Main Ideas and Listen for Details	16–17
11	Talk About the Topic, Parts A and B	18
12	Take the Unit Test	19
13	Extend the Topic, Part A	20
UNIT 3		
14	Build Your Vocabulary	23
15	Try It Out!	25
16	Listen for Main Ideas and Listen for Details	26–27
17	Talk About the Topic, Parts A and B	28
18	Take the Unit Test	29
19	Extend the Topic, Part A	30
UNIT 4		
20	Build Your Vocabulary	33
21	Try It Out!	35
22	Listen for Main Ideas and Listen for Details	36–37
23	Talk About the Topic, Parts A and B	38
24	Take the Unit Test	39
25	Extend the Topic, Part A	40

TRACK	ACTIVITY	PAGE
CD 2		
1	Introduction	
UNIT 5		
2	Build Your Vocabulary	43
3	Try It Out!	45
4	Listen for Main Ideas and Listen for Details	46–47
5	Talk About the Topic, Parts A and B	48
6	Take the Unit Test	49
7	Extend the Topic, Part A	50
UNIT 6		
8	Build Your Vocabulary	53
9	Try It Out!	55
10	Listen for Main Ideas and Listen for Details	56–57
11	Talk About the Topic, Parts A and B	58
12	Take the Unit Test	59
13	Extend the Topic, Part A	60
UNIT 7		
14	Build Your Vocabulary	63
15	Try It Out!	65
16	Listen for Main Ideas and Listen for Details	66–67
17	Talk About the Topic, Parts A and B	68
18	Take the Unit Test	69
19	Extend the Topic, Part A	70
UNIT 8		
20	Build Your Vocabulary	73
21	Try It Out!	75
22	Listen for Main Ideas and Listen for Details	76–77
23	Talk About the Topic, Parts A and B	78
24	Take the Unit Test	79
25	Extend the Topic, Part A	80

TRACK	ACTIVITY	PAGE
CD 3		
1	Introduction	
UNIT 9		
2	Build Your Vocabulary	83
3	Try It Out!	85
4	Listen for Main Ideas and Listen for Details	86–87
5	Talk About the Topic, Parts A and B	88
6	Take the Unit Test	89
7	Extend the Topic, Part A	90
UNIT 10		
8	Build Your Vocabulary	93
9	Try It Out!	95
10	Listen for Main Ideas and Listen for Details	96–97
11	Talk About the Topic, Parts A and B	98
12	Take the Unit Test	99
13	Extend the Topic, Part A	100
UNIT 11		
14	Build Your Vocabulary	103
15	Try It Out!	105
16	Listen for Main Ideas and Listen for Details	106–107
17	Talk About the Topic, Parts A and B	108
18	Take the Unit Test	109
19	Extend the Topic, Part A	110
UNIT 12		
20	Build Your Vocabulary	113
21	Try It Out!	115
22	Listen for Main Ideas and Listen for Details	116–117
23	Talk About the Topic, Parts A and B	118
24	Take the Unit Test	119
25	Extend the Topic, Part A	120

DVD: tracking guide

UNIT	FEATURE	STUDENT BOOK ACTIVITY

1	Lecture
	  Coaching Tips
	  Presentation Points
	Student Discussion
		Listen for Main Ideas and Listen for Details, pages 6–7
		
		Talk About the Topic, Parts A and B, page 8

2	Lecture
	  Coaching Tips
	  Presentation Points
	Student Discussion
		Listen for Main Ideas and Listen for Details, pages 16–17
		
		Talk About the Topic, Parts A and B, page 18

3	Lecture
	  Coaching Tips
	  Presentation Points
	Student Discussion
		Listen for Main Ideas and Listen for Details, pages 26–27
		
		Talk About the Topic, Parts A and B, page 28

4	Lecture
	  Coaching Tips
	  Presentation Points
	Student Discussion
		Listen for Main Ideas and Listen for Details, pages 36–37
		
		Talk About the Topic, Parts A and B, page 38

5	Lecture
	  Coaching Tips
	  Presentation Points
	Student Discussion
		Listen for Main Ideas and Listen for Details, pages 46–47
		
		Talk About the Topic, Parts A and B, page 48

6	Lecture
	  Coaching Tips
	  Presentation Points
	Student Discussion
		Listen for Main Ideas and Listen for Details, pages 56–57
		
		Talk About the Topic, Parts A and B, page 58

UNIT	FEATURE	STUDENT BOOK ACTIVITY
7		

	Lecture
	  Coaching Tips
	  Presentation Points
		Listen for Main Ideas and Listen for Details, pages 66–67

	Student Discussion	Talk About the Topic, Parts A and B, page 68
8		

	Lecture
	  Coaching Tips
	  Presentation Points
		Listen for Main Ideas and Listen for Details, pages 76–77

	Student Discussion	Talk About the Topic, Parts A and B, page 78
9		

	Lecture
	  Coaching Tips
	  Presentation Points
		Listen for Main Ideas and Listen for Details, pages 86–87

	Student Discussion	Talk About the Topic, Parts A and B, page 88
10		

	Lecture
	  Coaching Tips
	  Presentation Points
		Listen for Main Ideas and Listen for Details, pages 96–97

	Student Discussion	Talk About the Topic, Parts A and B, page 98
11		

	Lecture
	  Coaching Tips
	  Presentation Points
		Listen for Main Ideas and Listen for Details, pages 106–107

	Student Discussion	Talk About the Topic, Parts A and B, page 108
12		

	Lecture
	  Coaching Tips
	  Presentation Points
		Listen for Main Ideas and Listen for Details, pages 116–117

	Student Discussion	Talk About the Topic, Parts A and B, page 118